UNDERSTANDING
ADRIENNE RICH

UNDERSTANDING CONTEMPORARY AMERICAN LITERATURE
Matthew J. Bruccoli, Founding Editor
Linda Wagner-Martin, Series Editor

Also of Interest

UNDERSTANDING

ADRIENNE RICH

Jeannette E. Riley

THE UNIVERSITY OF
SOUTH CAROLINA PRESS

Hardcover and ebook editions published 2016
Paperback edition published 2024 by the University of South Carolina Press
Columbia, South Carolina 29208

uscpress.com

Printed in the United States of America

Library of Congress Cataloging-in-Publication Data
can be found at http://catalog.loc.gov/

ISBN: 978-1-61117-699-5 (hardcover)
ISBN: 978-1-64336-526-8 (paperback)
ISBN: 978-1-61117-700-8 (ebook)

This book would not have been written without the support of the women who have mentored me throughout my life: my mother, Liz Riley, who taught me to love words and reading; Minrose Gwin, for introducing me to Adrienne Rich and guiding my development as a reader of poetry; Ruth Salvaggio, for engaging me in the study of language and its power; Magali Carrera, for pushing me to write this book and for exemplifying how writing is essential to what we do; and Kathleen Torrens, for her keen editing eye and insightful comments along the (long) way.

Thank you to the Estate of Adrienne Rich and Claire Reinersten at W. W. Norton & Company, Inc., for assistance with permissions.

We must use what we have to invent what we desire.

Adrienne Rich, *What Is Found There:*
Notebooks on Poetry and Politics

CONTENTS

SERIES EDITOR'S PREFACE

The Understanding Contemporary American Literature series was founded by the estimable Matthew J. Bruccoli (1931–2008), who envisioned these volumes as guides or companions for students as well as good nonacademic readers, a legacy that will continue as new volumes are developed to fill in gaps among the over one hundred series volumes published to date and to embrace a host of new writers only now making their marks on our literature.

As Professor Bruccoli explained in his preface to the volumes he edited, because much influential contemporary literature makes special demands, "the word understanding in the titles was chosen deliberately. Many willing readers lack an adequate understanding of how contemporary literature works; that is, of what the author is attempting to express and the means by which it is conveyed." Aimed at fostering this understanding of good literature and good writers, the criticism and analysis in the series provide instruction in how to read certain contemporary writers—explicating their material, language, structures, themes, and perspectives—and facilitate a more profitable experience of the works under discussion.

In the twenty-first century Professor Bruccoli's prescience gives us an avenue to publish expert critiques of significant contemporary American writing. The series continues to map the literary landscape and to provide both instruction and enjoyment. Future volumes will seek to introduce new voices alongside canonized favorites, to chronicle the changing literature of our times, and to remain, as Professor Bruccoli conceived, contemporary in the best sense of the word.

Linda Wagner-Martin, Series Editor

PREFACE

For more than sixty years Adrienne Rich mapped who we are and what we believe in five essay collections, nineteen poetry collections, and four editions of collected poems. Her volumes of writings address a diverse range of issues including gender, class, sexuality, nationalism, poverty, violence, racism, and our individual and collective responsibilities to our local, national, and international communities. In doing so, she emerged as not just one of the foremost women writers in the United States but also as one of our foremost American poets. She is often cited as one of the most important poets of the post–World War II era, "one of [the] foremost feminist theorists of our time," a groundbreaking poet who has shaped our understandings of political and social movements, particularly the women's movement, since the 1960s and a powerful essayist who has consistently examined the intersections of poetry and politics (Meese, "Adrienne Rich" 232). Over her lifetime Rich received numerous awards, including two Guggenheim Fellowships, the Ruth Lilly Poetry Prize, the National Book Award, the Frost Silver Medal for Lifetime Achievement in Poetry, the Fellowship of the Academy of American Poets, the National Medal of the Arts, the Lenore Marshal/*Nation* Prize for Poetry, the Lambda Book Award, and the Fund for Human Dignity Award of the National Gay Task Force (Yorke 2). And this list is by no means complete.

There are more than three hundred articles published on Rich's work documenting the course of her career and investigating the development of her poetics. This fact alone speaks to her impact in American letters. A review of representative comments speaks powerfully to Rich's influence as well. Nadine Gordimer has claimed Rich as the "Blake of American letters" (Yorke 3). Judith McDaniel's 1978 essay outlines how "no poet's voice has spoken as hers has in this period of profound social change in the relations between women and men, amongst women themselves. In the nearly three decades in which Adrienne Rich has been writing poetry, the quality of her vision and of her poems has been unique" (321). In a brief review, "Exemplary Poet," the critic Rafael Campo comments on how Rich's poetry is "stunning in its originality" and that it is an "awe-inspiring work in progress, unafraid of the kind of conflict that engenders truth" (43). Helen Vendler, who has often written about Rich's work, finds that "the value of Rich's poems, ethically speaking, is that they have continued to press against insoluble questions of suffering, evil, love, justice, and patriotism" (223).

Alice Templeton, in "Contradictions: Tracking Adrienne Rich's Poetry," offers this assessment: "Adrienne Rich's poetry has always raised important, difficult questions about the cultural uses of poetry and the ideology of poetic and critical tradition. For over forty years her work has provided the occasion for critics to comment on the art of poetry, its political significance, the character of poetic tradition, and the value of poetry as a critical and creative cultural activity" (333). In a review of Rich's 1995 collection, *Dark Fields of the Republic: Poems 1991–1995*, the critic David St. John asserts, "It would be hard to overstate [Adrienne] Rich's influence as a cultural presence. There is no one whose poetry has spoken more eloquently for the oppressed and marginalized in America, no one who has more compassionately charted the course of individual human suffering across the horrifying and impersonal graph of recent history. Rich's extraordinary essays, as everyone must know by now, continue to be essential writings in the ongoing feminist struggle in this country and throughout the world." In her later career, Rich moved beyond feminist concerns to assume a Whitmanesque role assaying American culture and politics at the turn of the twenty-first century. As Mark Doty suggests, "In Adrienne Rich's strong hands, the poem is an instrument for change, if we can see into the structures of power and take on the work of making a dream—'the dream of a common language'—an actuality. As Whitman did, she calls us toward the country we could be, though she insists we acknowledge the country we are" (44).

Adrienne Rich died on March 27, 2012. The response, nationally and internationally, to this loss was immediate and speaks further to her place and import in American literature and culture. As Katha Pollit wrote, "The death of Adrienne Rich marks not only the end of a long and transcendent literary career—thirty books of poetry and prose, prizes beyond counting—but the end of a kind of poetry that mattered in the world beyond poetry." Pollit further commented that Rich "took on our gravest perplexities and injustices—inequality of race and gender and sexuality and class, war and its consequences, the despoiling of nature and language—and asked the biggest question about them: Who would we be if we could change our world?" Eavan Boland, the prominent Irish poet, asserted that "what Rich drew out of the shadows, and put into practice, was that deeply democratic, beautifully mixed alloy practiced by Whitman, and loved by the early Yeats, both frowned on by a later anti-populist mode. In her time, quite simply, she re-united the public poem with the political one. It is an enormous achievement." The Poetry Foundation claimed Rich as "one of America's foremost public intellectuals," while the *New York Times* wrote that Rich was "a poet of towering reputation and towering rage, whose work—distinguished by an unswerving progressive vision and a dazzling, empathic ferocity—brought the oppression of women and lesbians to the forefront of poetic discourse and kept it there for nearly a half-century" (Fox).

David Orr, also in the *New York Times,* noted that while Rich "was indeed an inspiring cultural force, she was at bottom a writer of poems. And the defiant political stands for which she became famous are entirely consistent with that identity and its long American heritage." According to W. W. Norton's Judith Pamplin, Rich's poetry and ideas "could change people's lives"; further, Rich was a "brilliant poet whose precision in word choice may be unparalleled, and "Adrienne wrote with a rare and unwavering integrity about social injustice and her influence in this wider sphere cannot be underestimated" (Flood). As Pollit stated, "Rich's career reminds us that poetry can be more than aesthetic, more than lyrics of personal feeling—although she wrote many beautiful lyrics. It can engage with the biggest issues of its day and speak to a large and passionate readership."

Understanding Adrienne Rich offers an exploration of Rich's long career. Out of necessity, this book provides a chronological analysis of Rich's work to track her poetic development from reserved, formalist poet to feminist visionary to citizen poet. The readings of the poems are grounded by Rich's prose. Thus the book not only gives an introduction for the new reader of Adrienne Rich's poetry and essays but also provides a returning reader with an overview of the development of an important American voice. At the same time, given the scope of Rich's wide-ranging career, this study is neither exhaustive nor conclusive.

ABBREVIATIONS

ADW	*An Atlas of the Difficult World, Poems 1988–1991*
BBP	*Blood, Bread, and Poetry: Selected Prose 1979–1985*
CEP	*Collected Early Poems: 1950–1970*
DCL	*The Dream of a Common Language: Poems 1974–1977*
DF	*Dark Fields of the Republic, Poems 1991–1995*
DW	*Diving into the Wreck: Poems 1971–1972*
LSS	*On Lies, Secrets, and Silence: Selected Prose 1966–1978*
MS	*Midnight Salvage: Poems 1995–1998*
OWB	*Of Woman Born: Motherhood as Experience and Institution*
SAR	*The School among the Ruins: Poems 2000–2004*
TNP	*Tonight No Poetry Will Serve: Poems 2007–2010*
TRL	*Telephone Ringing in the Labyrinth: Poems 2004–2006*
YNL	*Your Native Land, Your Life*
WFT	*What Is Found There: Notebooks on Poetry and Politics*
WP	*A Wild Patience Has Taken Me This Far: Poems 1978–1981*

CHAPTER 1

Understanding Adrienne Rich

Rich's long career can be viewed through three major sections: the writings of 1951 through 1971;* the writings of 1973 through 1985;† and the writings of 1986 to 2012.‡ Much of the path of Rich's early career, which encompassed her first seven collections of poetry, worked to expose the tensions she experienced during her early adult life as she sought to find her voice and subject matter. In 1963 *Snapshots of a Daughter-in-Law* emerged as a transitional volume that began to establish Rich's feminist voice and move her writing away from its formalist roots. The next phase of Rich's career emerged with *Diving into the Wreck* (1973), which established Rich's growing focus on women's history and movement, a focus that developed not only in her poetry but also through her prose collections. Throughout her writings from the 1970s into the 1980s, Rich examined women's history, sexuality, patriarchy, and politics through a widening feminist lens. In particular, the 1978 collection *The Dream of a Common Language* marked the emergence of a newly discovered and created voice. This collection moved Rich fully into a women-centered, process-oriented vision. *The Dream of a Common Language*, which contains the "Twenty-one Love

A Change of World (1951); *The Diamond Cutters* (1955); *Snapshots of a Daughter-in-Law* (1963); *Necessities of Life* (1966); *Leaflets* (1969); *The Will to Change* (1971).

†*Diving into the Wreck* (1973); *Poems: Selected and New* (1974); *Of Woman Born: Motherhood as Experience and Institution* (1976); *The Dream of a Common Language* (1977); *A Wild Patience Has Taken Me This Far* (1981); *The Fact of a Doorframe: Poems Selected and New 1950–1984* (1984).

‡*Your Native Land, Your Life* (1986); *Time's Power* (1988); *An Atlas of the Difficult World* (1991); *Dark Fields of the Republic* (1995); *Midnight Salvage* (1999); *Fox: Poems 1998–2000* (2003); *The School among the Ruins* (2006); *Telephone Ringing in the Labyrinth* (2009); *Tonight No Poetry Will Serve* (2011).

Poems" sequence, provides a sharp break from Rich's previous work as it explores women's roles in history and women's relationships with women. Rich stated that there is "a whole new poetry beginning here" (DCL 76).

From the early 1980s onward, Rich's work grew increasingly political in nature as she delved into the cultural traditions, governmental practices, and individual and communal identities that influenced not just her self-identity but also her understanding of how power exists, particularly the power of language. In these later works, Rich's poems call upon readers to take on responsibility for cultural oppressions and injustices, while also furthering Rich's investigation of how language inscribes meaning and plays an essential role in (re-)creating democracy. Further, much of Rich's work, overall, emerged from her focus on body politics and the search for an understanding of her identity, which she outlines fully in the 1984 essay "Notes toward a Politics of Location." There she states that "the need to begin with the female body—our own—was understood not as applying a Marxist principle *to* women, but as locating the grounds from which to speak with authority *as* women. . . . To reconnect our thinking and speaking with the body of this particular living individual, a woman" (BBP 213). Throughout her career poems offered representations of the gendered body, the sexualized body, the nationalized body, and the aging body to embody her feminist, liberatory poetics. Through this embodiment of a feminist poetics, Rich shapes readers and moves them to question and consider what could be possible in the world, while also demonstrating how one's identity forms and shifts in response to the worlds around us.

Rich's search for identity rests on her understanding that one's identity originates in the body and is consistently shifting depending on one's location and experiences. Consider a well-known statement by Rich: "As a woman I have a country; as a woman I cannot divest myself of that country merely by condemning its government or by saying three times 'As a woman my country is the whole world.' Tribal loyalties aside, and even if nation-states are now just pretexts used by multinational conglomerates to serve their interests, I need to understand how a place on the map is also a place in history within which as a woman, a Jew, a lesbian, a feminist I am created and trying to create" (BBP 212). Rich's statement marks the multiple identities she carried—identities shaped by gender, religion, sexuality, and nation. Rich realized the need to "begin, though, not with a continent or a country or a house, but with the geography closest in—the body" (BBP 212).

This body is immediately marked upon birth. As Rich recounts, when she was born in Baltimore, Maryland, in 1929, she was "defined as white before I was defined as female," and from "the outset that body had more than one identity" (BBP 215). Rich's historical context, the politics that existed within the location she occupied as a child, located her by her "color and sex as surely as a Black child was located by color and sex" (BBP 215). However, for Rich, that location carried "implications of white identity" that "were mystified by the presumption that white people are the center of [the] universe" (BBP 215). As an adult, Rich recognized that understanding her politics of location also meant being accountable for the power that different subject positions carry. She writes, "To locate myself in my body means more than understanding what it has meant to me to have a vulva and clitoris and uterus and breasts. It means recognizing this white skin, the places it has taken me, the places it has not let me go" (BBP 215–16).

Furthermore, Rich recognized the difference between writing "the body" versus writing "my body": "To write 'my body' plunges me into lived experience, particularity: I see scars, disfigurements, discolorations, damages, losses, as well as what pleases me. . . . To say 'the body' lifts me away from what has given me a primary perspective. To say 'my body' reduces the temptation to grandiose assertions" (BBP 215). As Rich notes, "my body" leads to lived experience; moreover, within this lived experience is an ongoing exploration of identity and self in relation to the world. In *Volatile Bodies,* Elizabeth Grosz writes, "If bodies are objects or things, they are like no others, for they are the centers of perspective, insight, reflection, desire, agency" (xi). Rich's poems investigate the body in its myriad forms; in doing so, as Mary Eagleton explains in "Adrienne Rich, Location and the Body," Rich demonstrates how "we are all located in multiple ways; these locations interconnect with intricate patternings; and, though certain locations may be to the fore at specific moments, a whole range of determining factors will always be operating" (330). In *What Is Found There: Notebooks on Poetry and Politics,* Rich writes, "That to track your own desire, in your own language, is not an isolated task. You yourself are marked by family, gender, caste, landscape, the struggle to make a living, or the absence of such a struggle. The rich and the poor are equally marked. Poetry is never free of these markings even when it appears to be. Look into the images" (216). Throughout her work, Rich delves into images that reveal the body's markings to consider how these markings create our politics.

Rich's development as a poet, as well as her examination of how identity is shaped by our experiences, was rooted in her family background. Born in Baltimore, Maryland, on May 16, 1929, to a Jewish father and a Protestant mother, Rich had an early life that was marked by tension and conflict. In the poem "Readings of History" two of Rich's lines emerge as a clear marker of the underlying concerns that dominate much of her early work and remain one of the major themes in her later work: "Split at the root, neither Gentile nor Jew, / Yankee nor Rebel" (CEP 164). Rich as early as 1960 recognized that certain oppositions shaped her ever-fluctuating identities. In these particular lines, written when Rich was thirty-one years old and living in Cambridge, Massachusetts, as a young mother and wife, Rich confronts her Jewish heritage from her father and her Protestant upbringing from her mother as well as her adolescence in the South and her college days and early married life in the North.

In order to understand how these conflicts influenced Rich's work, we need to start with the world she was born into: Baltimore, Maryland, at the end of the 1920s. Rich's father, Dr. Arnold Rich, was a pathologist and professor at Johns Hopkins University, and her mother, Helen Jones Rich, was a career wife and mother despite her early training as a concert pianist and composer. In "Split at the Root: An Essay on Jewish Identity," Rich points out that her feelings of being split and facing endless oppositions began in the hospital where she was born, her "father's workplace, a hospital in the Black ghetto, whose lobby contained an immense white marble statue of Christ" (BBP 101). She explains that the world she entered was a Christian one—a world based on and made in response to Christian values, imagery, language, and assumptions: "The world of acceptable folk was white, gentile (christian, really), and had 'ideals' (which colored people, white 'common' people, were not supposed to have). 'Ideals' and 'manners' included not hurting someone's feelings by calling her or him a Negro or a Jew—naming the hated identity. This is the mental framework of the 1930s and 1940s in which I was raised" (BBP 104). The mental framework of Rich's early childhood and adolescence was further complicated by her father's Jewishness, long denied and ignored, and her mother's Protestantism. For Rich, even bringing up the issues of religion, race, and class caused concern and worry as she looked back in 1982 on her early years: "Writing this, I feel dimly like the betrayer: of my father, who did not speak the word; of my mother, who must have trained me in the messages; of my caste and class; of my whiteness itself" (BBP 104).

Even in her childhood, Rich felt the tension of split identities—first through religion and then, later on, through her own positions as wife, mother, heterosexual, lesbian, feminist, Jew, poet, and woman. The tension at times caused Rich to yearn to rid herself of certain aspects of her identity, yet she also realized the difficulties of such an action: "It would be easy to push away and deny the gentile in me—that white southern woman, that social christian. At different times in my life I have wanted to push away one or the other burden of inheritance, to say merely *I am a woman; I am a lesbian.* If I call myself a Jewish lesbian, do I thereby try to shed some of my southern gentile white woman's culpability? If I call myself only through my mother, is it because I pass more easily through a world where being a lesbian often seems like outsiderhood enough?" (BBP 103). Shedding one aspect of her identity merely created other conflicts; for example, dropping the identifier of Gentile forced her to confront her Jewish inheritance, while dropping the identifier of lesbian forced her to accept the culpability inherent in the southern white woman's position she inherited from her mother.

However, while Rich's parents remained silent and complicit in the on-going Christian ideals as well as the societal conflicts and expectations that dominated Rich's world, they also encouraged her to read and write, and she was immediately directed toward the study of poetry. Educated at home by her mother until the fourth grade under the watchful eye of her demanding father, Rich learned about poetry by copying the works of poets such as Blake and Yeats over and over again as well as by immersing herself in her father's library. Her father, as she writes in "Split at the Root," "was an amateur musician, read poetry, adored encyclopedic knowledge. He prowled and pounced over my school papers, insisting I use 'grown-up' sources; he criticized my poems for faulty technique and gave me books on rhyme and meter and form" (BBP 113). While Rich recounts that his oversight was "egotistical, tyrannical, opin-ionated, and terribly wearing," she also notes how he taught her to "believe in hard work, to mistrust easy inspiration, to write and rewrite; to feel that I *was* a person of the book, even though a woman; to take ideas seriously" (BBP 113). Most importantly, Rich states, he made her "feel, at a very young age, the power of language and that [she] could share in it" (BBP 113).

The poem "Juvenilia," from *Snapshots of a Daughter-in-Law,* recounts Rich's struggle with her father as the poem presents the picture of a young child sitting "under duress" at her father's desk copying poems. As the poem unfolds, the child's action of "stabbing the blotting-pad" as "Unspeakable fairy tales ebb like blood through [her] head" suggests her uneasiness with her father's overbearing presence and the requirement that she copy the male masters who have preceded her (CEP 156). Reflecting back in her 1971 essay "When We Dead Awaken: Writing as Revision," Rich recognizes the influence her father held over her work and how she "tried for a long time to please him, or rather, not to displease him" (LSS 38). The influence of male writers on her work raised another tension: "And then of course there were other men—writers, teachers—the Man, who was not a terror or a dream but a literary master and master in other ways less easy to acknowledge" (LSS 39). This tension was exacerbated by the recognition that "there were all those poems about women, written by men: it seemed to be a given that men wrote poems and women frequently inhabited them" (LSS 39).

At the same time, the schooling paid off. Rich attended Radcliffe College, graduating in 1951, the same year her first book of poetry, *A Change of World,* appeared. This book received the Yale Series of Younger Poets Award. In later years Rich would say that she "published [her] first book by a fluke" (LSS 42). Auden's famous comments about the volume, praising the poems because they are "neatly and modestly dressed, speak quietly but do not mumble, respect their elders but are not cowed by them, and do not tell fibs," have often been quoted by critics, feminists in particular, as a patriarchal downplaying of Rich's poetic talent (Auden 278–79). Nevertheless, Auden's words of praise act appropriately as an introduction to a volume of poetry that exhibits fine craftsmanship drawn from the imitation of the styles of male poet precursors through formula poems and allusions that play upon oppositions and the innocent hope to find a "better" world—hence the title *A Change of World*.

Terrence Des Pres explains in his article "Adrienne Rich, North America East" (1988) that "Adrienne Rich didn't start a leader. Her early work, praised by Auden and Randall Jarrell among others, shows her the dutiful daughter of the fathers, Auden and Jarrell among them" (192). However, while the poems found in *A Change of World* echo the forms of male poets, upon closer reading they also suggest more than simply a dutiful daughter of the fathers. Adalaide Morris points out that, when asked about her first volume of poems, Rich stated that the craft lay not in the strict attention to detail and imitation of male formalism but rather in the "act of covering" (137). Morris goes on to explain that "because its language functioned less to discover than to display, the words worked, in her image, "more as a kind of facade than as either self-revelation or as a probe into one's own consciousness." The facade is an excellent image for these architecturally intricate and static poems, poems whose elegantly undisrupted exposition seems to conceal as much as it reveals" (137).

The poems do tend to conceal as much as they reveal. *A Change of World* offers glimpses of the voice we now associate with Adrienne Rich, one of our foremost contemporary American poets. The poems offer traces of confidence, concerns with women's roles, and the powers of language under the seemingly "modest" surface of poems that "do not tell fibs" (Auden 277). Rich discusses the beginnings of that voice in her essay "When We Dead Awaken: Writing as Revision": "I know that my style was formed first by male poets; [. . .] Frost, Dylan Thomas, Donne, Auden, MacNeice, Stevens, Yeats. What I chiefly learned from them was craft. But poems are like dreams: in them you put what you don't know you know. Looking back at poems I wrote before I was twenty-one, I am startled because beneath the conscious craft are glimpses of the split I even then experienced between the girl who wrote poems, who defined herself in writing poems, and the girl who was to define herself by her relationships with men" (LSS 39–40). This acknowledgment of the "girl who wrote poems, who defined herself in writing poems, and the girl who was to define herself by her relationships with men" marks the beginnings of Rich's mature poetic voice.

Not surprisingly, *A Change of World* contains only three out of forty poems that have a woman as their primary subject: "Aunt Jennifer's Tigers"; "An Unsaid Word"; and "Mathilde in Normandy." Knowing that poetry was "supposed" to be male, that women were not "supposed" to write poetry, Rich played by the rules set up by male literary precursors. She clearly explains the inevitability of her following the rules in her essay "The Location of the Poet": "I took what I could use where I could find it. When the ideas or forms we need are banished, we seek their residues wherever we can trace them. But there was one major problem with this. I had been born a woman, and I was trying to think and act as if poetry—and the possibility of making poems— were a universal—a gender-neutral—realm" (BBP 174–75). As a young poet, Rich found herself conditioned to use what she was most familiar with: the ideas and subject matter of "the Man, who was not a terror or a dream but a literary master and a master in other ways less easy to acknowledge" (LSS 39). Even reading women poets did not resolve Rich's concerns as she found herself seeking what she saw in men's poetry as she did not yet understand that to be equal did not mean sounding the same (LSS 39). In order to understand the conflicts present in Rich's early voice, we need only to turn to the often-anthologized poem "Storm Warnings," which opens *A Change of World.*

"Storm Warnings" juxtaposes an encroaching storm and the emotions of an individual safely protected inside a house. The individual remains gender neutral as Rich employs the universal "I" that becomes "We" later in the poem, thus modeling the formalist tradition in which she was trained. In doing so, she follows T. S. Eliot's belief that the poet has "not a 'personality' to express, but a particular medium, which is only a medium and not a personality" (42). Furthermore, Rich's avoidance of a personal "I" also reflects Eliot's belief that "poetry is not a turning loose of emotion, but an escape from emotion; it is not the expression of personality, but an escape from personality" (43).

The poem begins with a change in pressure witnessed by the barometer and the speaker in the poem as a storm approaches. The poem's speaker realizes, unlike the inanimate instrument that predicts weather change, the approaching danger. At the same time, the speaker recognizes the safety that windows offer and the futility of hoping to change the weather pattern, for as the second stanza reveals, "Weather abroad / And weather in the heart alike come on / Regardless of prediction" (CEP 3). The coming weather, like the emotions of the heart, cannot be thwarted since each force follows its own timetable and path.

The speaker questions the individual's inability to avoid the turmoil of such storms of weather and emotion in the third stanza: "Between foreseeing and averting change / Lies all the mastery of elements" that no weather instruments can change since "Time in the hand is not control" (CEP 3). The word "change" stands out as the key word of this stanza and the poem, for change cannot be foreseen or averted. Like a hand holding a watch cannot control time, the instruments that predict changing weather offer neither protection nor defense against coming storms. The sole safety lies in our ability to "only close the shutters" (CEP 3), and the speaker "draw[s] the curtains as the sky goes black" (CEP 3). At the same time, the speaker lights "candles sheathed in glass," while the storm, with an "insistent whine," pushes "Against the keyhold draught" (CEP 3). The poem draws to a close with the speaker attempting to reconcile the storm's presence and the dangers it poses: "This is our sole defense against the season; / These are the things that we have learned to do / Who live in troubled regions" (CEP 3). The windows, shutters, curtains, light from candles protected by glass, and walls of the building provide the "sole defense" against the outer elements. The individual, forced to withdraw from the oncoming storm, believes that safety has been located through enclosure within the room.

Yet while the poem plays upon the desire for protection from a dangerous world that can neither be predicted nor avoided, as Morris points out, "the solution, though boldly stated, seems uneasy, for the poem's imagery suggests that the protagonist has locked the door with the threat inside" (144). Morris further asserts that the room suggests a self-created "entombment" that is avoided only since the aperture in the keyhole remains unsealed (144). Here, Rich relies on a set of oppositions to create her ideas: inside vs. outside; safety vs. danger; man-made structures vs. nature. Each opposition enacts tensions Rich feels as a woman and a poet. Her roles as wife and mother, caretaking positions, oppose her role as a poet, an artistic and active position. According to Rich, this opposition occupies many women's lives, for the "twentieth-century, educated young woman, looking perhaps at her mother's life, or trying to create an autonomous self in a society which insists that she is destined primarily for reproduction, has with good reason felt that the choice was an inescapable either/or: motherhood or individuation, motherhood or creativity, motherhood or freedom" (OWB 160). Yet seemingly there is no escape at this time for Rich; while she struggles for answers and a region that is less troubled and stormy than the one she currently inhabits, she has yet to discover a resolution to the dueling identities within her.

This struggle is also seen in the second poem of the collection, "Aunt Jennifer's Tigers," which is often cited by feminists as a marker of Rich's later feminist voice. In the poem Rich reveals the split she felt between the girl who defined herself in relationship to men and the girl who wrote poetry. In order to reveal that split, Rich still maintains a formalist pose, employing a set rhyme scheme (aabb) in the three quatrains that make up the poem. Yet by demonstrating strong craftsmanship that actually mimics the trapped position of Aunt Jennifer in her own life, Rich inserted the beginnings of her concerns with women's positions as objects in society and in poetic language.

The plot of the poem is clear: Aunt Jennifer stitches the images of tigers, who "pace in sleek chivalric certainty," on a screen. The image of the tigers' freedom, confidence, and lack of fear stands in direct opposition to the emotions of Aunt Jennifer as "The massive weight of Uncle's wedding band / Sits heavily upon Aunt Jennifer's hand" (CEP 4). The poem concludes noting that once Aunt Jennifer is dead, her "terrified hands will lie / Still ringed with ordeals she was mastered by" (CEP 4); meanwhile the tigers "in the panel that she made / Will go on prancing, proud and unafraid" (CEP 4). Attempting to create something of her own, Aunt Jennifer finds that the needle is extremely hard to pull as the band represents the weight of the marriage and society's expectations of women suffocating her life. What remains as the poem concludes is an image of the tigers still prancing, while Aunt Jennifer is "mastered by" the rings of her life.

The well-anthologized "Aunt Jennifer's Tigers" is an early preview of the investigation of gender to come in Rich's body of work. The poem's depiction of Aunt Jennifer trapped in marriage, relegated to the domestic sphere, points to Rich's burgeoning questioning of gender roles. Even Aunt Jennifer's death, the poem suggests, does not free her from the patriarchal expectations and duties of marriage as she remains "still ringed with the ordeals she was mastered by" (CEP 4). In essence, Aunt Jennifer's fixed position in opposition to the tigers' freedom reveals the tension that exists between the "expected" roles for women in the 1950s and the desire of women such as Aunt Jennifer to have independence to pursue interests of their own. Such limits weigh her thread down and thwart her creative impulses so that when she dies she remains marked by her role as a wife and mother rather than her desire to create an art of her own. Betty Friedan's famous work, *The Feminine Mystique,* was groundbreaking in its discussion of the American housewife of the 1950s who was supposed to be "healthy, beautiful, educated, concerned only about her husband, her children, her home. She had found true feminine fulfillment. As a housewife and mother, she was respected as a full and equal partner to man in his world. She was free to choose automobiles, clothes, appliances, supermarkets; she had everything that women ever dreamed of" (Friedan 36). Yet as Aunt Jennifer's tapestry indicates, the vision of the American housewife left women unfulfilled and empty, if not "terrified."

Rich's well-structured verse calls into question the assumption that marriage brings happiness for women. Bound by patriarchal expectations, Aunt

Jennifer's world remains structured by the world of men. Yet while Aunt Jennifer's life is marked by the ordeals created in part by the feminine mystique, the tigers maintain freedom of movement on the panel that she made, suggesting the freedom of identity that Aunt Jennifer herself may desire. In inserting the tigers into the tapestry, Aunt Jennifer subtly yet effectively pleads for life outside of the structures established for her. Unfortunately, Aunt Jennifer remains able only to stitch freedom of movement and expressions of power in the shape of the tigers into a tapestry, an action that reveals her inability to make her own choices regarding her position in the world.

While the message in "Aunt Jennifer's Tigers" is neither positive nor sustaining for women in the long run, the poem emerged as the first concrete sign of Rich's gendered poetic identity. Although Rich was unable to have the woman in the poem act and speak in the first person, she still made a breakthrough as Aunt Jennifer acts and feels emotions in the poem. Even more specifically, Rich employed images of stitching—an act traditionally associated with women's artistry and read as a feminist strategy—to expose women's oppressed positions in a patriarchal society and the beginnings of women's resistance to such positions. Moreover, the act of sewing functions as a protective device, as well as a device for recovering losses from the past, as suggested by Sandra Gilbert and Susan Gubar in *The Madwoman in the Attic: The Woman Writer and the Nineteenth Century:* "Like Ariadne, Penelope, and Philomela, women have used their looms, thread, and needles both to defend themselves and silently to speak of themselves. Like Mary Shelley, gathering the Sibyl's scattered leaves in *The Last Man,* they have sewed to heal the wounds inflicted in history" (642). Aunt Jennifer's stitching not only preserves her own history but also calls into question the forces that relegated her to an insignificant position with little independence. Such use of a traditional female metaphor suggests Rich's unconscious desire to understand how gender impacts women's lives.

"Aunt Jennifer's Tigers" stands as one of Rich's strongest explorations of the oppositions that dominated her early adult life and acts as a marker of the work to come. Significantly, Rich cited "Aunt Jennifer's Tigers" in a 1991 interview with David Montenegro as one of eighteen poems she viewed as "landmarks of [her] development in her poetry" (Montenegro 17). Her reasons for this selection are explained more in the essay "When We Dead Awaken: Writing as Re-Vision," where she writes, "It was important to me that Aunt Jennifer was a person as distinct from myself as possible—distanced by the formalism of the poem, by its objective, observant tone—even by putting the woman in a different generation. In those years formalism was a part of the strategy—like asbestos gloves, it allowed me to handle materials I couldn't pick up barehanded"

(LSS 40–41). The training in formalism from her father's schooling allowed Rich to create the poem and infuse the stirrings of her concerns with women caught in a patriarchal world. Aunt Jennifer's ordeal, seemingly distinct and separate from Rich herself, represents the subject matter that would become the dominant concern in her later work.

Moreover, since Rich found herself at a loss when confronted by the different roles expected of her as a wife and mother, formalism provided Rich with the "tools" to handle material that was unfamiliar and frightening to her. She recounts in *Of Woman Born*, "I did not then understand that we—the women of that academic community—as in so many middle-class communities of the period—were expected to fill both the part of the Victorian Lady of Leisure, the Angel in the House, and also of the Victorian cook, scullery maid, laundress, governess, and nurse. I only sensed that there were false distractions sucking at me, and I wanted desperately to strip my life down to what was essential" (27–28). She purposefully created a woman distanced from her, encased in a rhyme scheme and tone of neutral observation, in order to move gently around issues and "false distractions" that stood in opposition to the roles she was expected to fulfill as a woman, as well as her own thoughts about the missing elements in her life.

The issues surrounding Rich's identities as a woman and a poet are reinforced by other renderings of opposing tensions in *A Change of World*. These dualisms depend on an either/or way of thinking and seeing the world and move beyond male/female relationships into larger spheres that encompass nature versus society, religion/structure versus anarchy/chaos, emotion versus love, and desire versus necessity, among others. For example, the poem "Boundary," the twentieth poem and located almost directly in the middle of the collection, stands as a marker of Rich's overall concern with a dualistic way of thinking and the way in which such thinking dominated her life. Recognizing that the world cannot easily be split in two, Rich still longed for a way of splitting the difference. As the poem concludes,

> There's enormity in a hair
> Enough to lead men not to share
> Narrow confines of a sphere
> But put an ocean or a fence
> Between two opposite intents.
> A hair would span the difference. (CEP 25)

The voice of the speaker of the poem remains detached and emotionless. We see a similar approach in other poems, such as "Air without Incense," where

Rich opposes the structure of religion against the disorder of chaos, and "At a Bach Concert," which portrays the oppositions of discipline versus emotion and desire versus necessity.

Furthermore, in a defense of the formalism she learned from the male-dominated literary past, Rich knew that "Form is the ultimate gift that love can offer" and that a "too-compassionate art is half an art" (CEP 30). Following poetic traditions before her, Rich created a collection of poetry that depicts tensions in her life as she struggled to locate her identity as both a woman and a poet in 1950s America. Under the guise of detachment and formalism, the early poems in *A Change of World* serve as an introduction to Rich's constant movement between the opposing identities of woman and poet bound by the formalist tradition. Paula Bennett's *My Life, a Loaded Gun: Female Creativity and Feminist Poetics* accurately summarizes Rich's early work: "Created by an author who presents her speaker as neither distinctively male nor distinctively female, who is without background or character, who exhibits neither lusts nor appetites, needs nor fears, and who writes above all in total unawareness of the physical self, the poems in Rich's first two volumes are the undiluted products of the tradition from which they derive" (183). Poems such as "For the Felling of an Elm in the Harvard Yard," which details the objectivity with which students view the loss of a centuries-old tree, and "Why Else But to Forestall This Hour," which unemotionally presents the picture of a man who has lived cautiously and carefully throughout his entire life, a man who "has outmisered death" and no longer wonders why he moves forward, continue the tradition set by poets, such as Yeats, whom Rich so admired (CEP 18).

As a result, while conflicts are apparent in her early work, the subject matter remains subdued, objective, and it lacks, as Bennett points out, "poetry written out of life," with a poem such as "Aunt Jennifer's Tigers" being the exception rather than the norm (181). Rich, in an interview with Stanley Plumly in 1971, understood the avoidance she enacted in her early work: "I was going through a very sort of female thing—of trying to distinguish between the ego that is capable of writing poems, and then this other kind of being that you're asked to be if you're a woman, who is, in a sense, denying that ego. I had great feelings of split about that for many years actually, and there are a lot of poems I couldn't write even, because I didn't want to confess to having that much aggression, that much ego, that much sense of myself. I had always thought of my first book as being a book of very well-tooled poems of a sort of very bright student, which I was at that time, but poems in which the unconscious things never got to the surface" (31). Unconscious or not, the splits that Rich spoke of continued to reveal themselves in her later work, revelations that began to emerge in her second and third collections, *The Diamond Cutters and Other Poems* (1955) and *Snapshots of a Daughter-in-Law* (1963).

Following the publication of *A Change of World,* with the support of a Guggenheim Fellowship, Rich spent 1952 traveling in Europe. Upon her return home, at the age of twenty-three, she married Alfred H. Conrad, a twenty-nine-year-old economist working at Harvard, and they settled in the Boston, Massachusetts, area. The marriage caused family tension as her parents refused to attend the wedding. As Rich recounts in "Split at the Root," "I was marrying a Jew of the 'wrong kind' from an Orthodox eastern European background. Brooklyn-born, he had gone to Harvard, changed his name," and her father "saw this marriage as my having fallen prey to the Jewish family, eastern European division" (BBP 114). Rich married, as many did during her generation in the 1950s, because she "knew no better way to disconnect" from her "first family" (BBP 115). She soon gave birth to her first son, David, in 1955, followed by her second son, Paul, in 1957 and her third son, Jacob, in 1959. A full-time mother, Rich still strove to write poetry. During this time Rich published *The Diamond Cutters and Other Poems* in 1955.

The poems follow in the tradition of *A Change of World* by remaining firmly formalistic, and as Claire Keyes explains in *The Aesthetics of Power: The Poetry of Adrienne Rich* (1986), the collection that emerged is "a book of traditional, male-influenced poems" and "provides little indication of [Rich's] later distinctiveness as a feminist poet" (30). Readers can hear echoes of Robert Frost in poems such as "Autumn Equinox" and "The Perennial Answer," while other poems, through an air of objectivity and distance, provide descriptions of places such as "Concord River," "A Walk by the Charles," and "A View of Merton College." Still other poems delve into the creation of art and the demands on the artist as seen in "Love in a Museum" and "Colophon."

The title poem provides a representative example of Rich's formal poetic techniques and her modernist, male-formed style drawn from poets such as Auden and Frost. The poem is driven by form as Rich uses iambic trimeters in five stanzas of eight lines each employing a short line that creates a firm, objective tone. The poem's speaker appears to be an experienced diamond cutter talking to an apprentice. The discussion of diamond cutting can be seen to offer a commentary on the act of creating art. The speaker cautions the novice about the challenge of the process, pointing out that the "stone may have contempt / For too-familiar hands" and that one must "Respect the adversary / Meet it with tools refined" (CEP 131). More importantly, the diamond cutter or artist must be "hard of heart" (CEP 131), as ultimately the work of art will leave the craftsperson's hands; thus the speaker states that one should "Love only what you do, / And not what you have done" (CEP 132). Throughout, the poem remains emotionally removed and passionless. Keyes reads this poem as one that puts forth "a traditional form of masculine power" (44) that creates "an inextricable connection between masculinity and the creative process" (45).

Randall Jarrell's review of *The Diamond Cutters and Other Poems* for the *Yale Review* in 1956 found Rich's second collection to be formally strong. Reminiscent of Auden's foreword to *A Change of World*, Jarrell concluded with the following pronouncement: "meanwhile, today, she is also an endearing and delightful poet, one who deserves Shakespeare's favorite adjective, *sweet*" (129). In another review Donald Hall commented that "precision and frequent profundity characterize the best of [Rich's] verse, a verse which can be rigorous and charming at the same time. The range within her work, the variety of tones and styles which she can assume, is the most promising of her characteristics" (213). Hall went on to hope that Rich "may extend the range of her performances still further" (213).

In retrospect, Rich was dissatisfied with her early work. In 1971 she reflected upon the time period in which she wrote *The Diamond Cutters and Other Poems:* "I went on trying to write; my second book and first child appeared in the same month. But by the time that book came out I was already dissatisfied with those poems, which seemed to me mere exercises for poems I hadn't written. The book was praised, however, for its 'gracefulness'; I had a marriage and a child. If there were doubts, if there were periods of null depression or active despairing, these could only mean that I was ungrateful, insatiable, perhaps a monster" (LSS 42). For Rich, the poems were "mere exercises," which is not surprising given her formalist training and the male-dominated literary tradition that guided that training. However, as Rich's comments also demonstrate, she was starting to question the roles she was expected to fulfill as wife and mother as she sought to create poems that expressed her thoughts as a woman.

According to Rich four years later in 1975 in her essay "Vesuvius at Home: The Power of Emily Dickinson," "It is an extremely painful and dangerous way to live—split between a publicly accepted persona, and a part of yourself that you perceive as the essential, the creative and powerful self, yet also as possibly unacceptable, perhaps even monstrous" (LSS 175). While Rich's poetry was recognized for its craftsmanship, the formal, objective lines and praise for being "sweet," "endearing," and "delightful" hide the actual conflicts that Rich the poet was facing (Jarrell 129). As a result of the tensions she felt as a mother and poet, Rich found herself unable to continue writing. Even more disturbing, as she wrote in a November 1956 journal entry, Rich found herself feeling "nothing but boredom and indifference" toward her work (OWB 26). Further, Rich wrote that when asked about her "career," she felt a "strong sense of wanting to deny all responsibility for and interest in that person who writes—or who wrote" (OWB 27).

Expecting her third child in 1958, Rich explained, again in retrospect in 1975, that at the time she felt she "had either to consider myself a failed woman and a failed poet, or to try to find some synthesis by which to understand what was happening to me. What frightened me most was the sense of drift, of being pulled along on a current which called itself my destiny, but in which I seemed to be losing touch with whoever I had been, with the girl who had experienced her own will and energy almost ecstatically at times, walking around a city or riding a train at night or typing in a student room" (LSS 42). Her efforts to understand what was happening to her and to find "clues" that would illuminate her position and identity led Rich finally, after years of "reading in fierce snatches, scribbling in notebooks, writing poetry in fragments," to a breakthrough with *Snapshots of a Daughter-in-Law,* which was published in 1963 after a silence of eight years (LSS 44).

CHAPTER 2

"A Life I didn't choose / chose me"

Transitions

Adrienne Rich's career is marked by significant transitional moments in her work. One occurred during the period of the publication of her third collection of poetry, *Snapshots of a Daughter-in-Law*, in 1963 and the subsequent collections *Necessities of Life* (1966), *Leaflets* (1969), and *The Will to Change* (1971). Significantly, *Snapshots* emerged after an eight-year silence from 1955 to 1963, a time when Rich found herself deeply occupied by her duties as a wife and a mother to three young boys and conflicted about her desire to write. Rich documents the challenges of this time period in *Of Woman Born: Motherhood as Experience and Institution* (1976), which interweaves journal entries with her analysis of her individual experience of motherhood as well as motherhood as a cultural institution.

In 1959 Rich experienced her third and final pregnancy after giving birth in 1955 and 1957. While the birth of a third child was welcome, Rich's journal entries also point to her growing dissatisfaction with motherhood as she sought time to "again be free, no longer so physically tired, pursuing a more or less intellectual and creative life" (OWB 28). Her desire to write conflicted with her expected roles as wife and mother. As Rich explains, "My husband was a sensitive, affectionate man who wanted children and who—unusual in the professional, academic world of the fifties—was willing to 'help.' But it was clearly understood that this 'help' was an act of generosity; that *his* work, *his* professional life, was the real work in the family; in fact, this was for years not even an issue between us. I understood that my struggles as a writer were a kind of luxury; a peculiarity of mine; my work brought in almost no money: it even cost money, when I hired a household helper to allow me a few hours a week to write" (OWB 27).

While she was struggling to find time to write, Rich saw herself as a burden: "I experienced my depressions, bursts of anger, sense of entrapment, as burdens my husband was forced to bear because he loved me; I felt grateful to be loved in spite of bringing him those burdens" (OWB 27). Caught in the trappings of domestic life "swarming with children" in the midst of "repetitious cycles of laundry, the night wakings, the interrupted moments of peace or of engagement with ideas, the ludicrous dinner parties," Rich found herself thinking that she "*knew* I had to remake" her life (OWB 27). In a 1958 journal entry, Rich pushes back against feelings of stagnation, recognizing that it is "really death that I have been fearing—the crumbling to death of that scarcely-born physiognomy which my whole life has been a battle to give birth to—a recognizable, autonomous self, a creation in poetry and in life" (OWB 29).

The creation of an autonomous self began to emerge in *Snapshots,* a collection with new material that handles, albeit cautiously, experiences of "real" life. Turning away from the woman haunted by her responsibilities as wife, mother, and daughter, Rich chose in *Snapshots* to bring to the surface the parts of herself that had been concealed behind the formalistic writing traditions she had followed. The lines of the poems are looser, more experimental, and many escape conventional forms. In 1964 Rich commented that the goals of her earlier poems were control, technical mastery, and intellectual clarity. However, she also explained that with *Snapshots* she was learning to write poems based on her growing sense of poetry as subjective rather than universal: "Perhaps a simple way of putting it would be to say that instead of poems *about* experiences I am getting poems that *are* experiences, that contribute to my knowledge and my emotional life even while they reflect and assimilate it" (Rich, "Poetry and Experience"). Her experiences as a woman required revising the male canonical form to ensure accurate expression of women's lives. Increasingly as Rich was finishing her third collection in 1963, she found herself moving back and forth between the experiences that made up her life at that point in time. The tensions between socially constructed roles for women and the objective, universal tone of the literary past began to form new poetry as Rich moved to merge her art and her life.

The second poem of the collection, "From Morning-Glory to Petersburg," exemplifies this new connection as it details a loss of innocence when one realizes that knowledge is neither pure nor simple. The poem works in two sections with varying line lengths and meters. The speaker reflects upon a romanticized memory of reading *The World Book* in childhood "when knowledge still was pure / not contradictory" and as "pleasurable / as cutting out a paper doll" (CEP 136). As the speaker recounts,

> You opened up a book and there it was:
> everything just as promised, from
> Kurdistan to Mormons, Gum
> Arabic to Kumquat, neither more nor less (CEP 136)

What made childhood possible, the speaker tells us, is that "facts could be kept separate / by a convention" (CEP 136).

The poem shifts into the second half as the speaker abruptly announces, "Now knowledge finds me out; / in all its risible untidiness" (CEP 136). Knowledge is messy, "dragging in things I never thought about" as "jeering irresponsibles always / comes along gypsy-style" (CEP 136). While the speaker longs to go backward to a simpler time, the poem ends with the acknowledgment that "it's too late" (CEP 136). In questioning what we hold to be knowledge, the poem presents a shift in Rich's work as she questions the subjective nature of knowledge formation.

We see in another poem later in *Snapshots of a Daughter-in-Law,* "Prospective Immigrants Please Note," Rich's recognition of the new and difficult position she now occupied. The speaker here confronts a complicated decision as the speaker needs to determine whether or not to move through a door. For the poem's speaker, there is a choice: "Either you will / go through this door / or you will not go through" (CEP 188). The choice is fraught with danger; if one goes through the door, s/he will be faced with the "risk / of remembering your name" (CEP 188). If the speaker chooses not to pass through the doorway, "it is possible / to live worthily // to maintain your attitudes / to hold your position" (CEP 188). Yet it is also possible that "much will blind you, / much will evade you," causing the speaker to ask, "at what cost who knows?" (CEP 188). The poem concludes with a final stanza with a door that "makes no promises" for "It is only a door" (CEP 188). Either decision, remaining safe inside or stepping out to the world, is risky. The poem suggests, however, that while risks are involved, failure to pass through the doorway will leave the speaker avoiding full engagement with the world.

In the end the poem "Prospective Immigrants Please Note" calls for doing away with indecisiveness and either/or dichotomies that endlessly present themselves. Moreover, passing through the doorway will change a person's life irrevocably, a point clearly made in Deborah Pope's *A Separate Vision: Isolation in Contemporary Women's Poetry:* "There can be no equivocation, no straddling of boundaries. On one side is safety, respectability, 'attitudes' and 'positions' but also the implication of illusion, evasion, and spiritual death. On the other side is the reality of self, but not without risk for those who have long harbored illusion. If one side is 'blind,' the other brings vision equally painful and the irrefutable status of an immigrant, a stranger, a pioneer in reality" (121). The question "at what cost who knows?" haunts the poem and implies that failure to pass through the door will greatly harm the individual. The poet must choose whether to break the bounds of tradition that entrap her.

Significantly the person who chooses to move forward, away from safety, becomes identified as an "immigrant." The location found beyond the doorway reduces both power and personal identity to that of a stranger with no claim to land or the language. Rich found herself in a similar position. Stepping through the doorway was part of Rich's search for a new path and an attempt to understand her position as a woman in 1960s North America. As she states in the poem "Double Monologue,"

> Since I was more than a child
>   trying on a thousand faces
> I have wanted one thing: to know
>   simply as I know my name
> at any given moment, where I stand. (CEP 157)

Rich's decision in *Snapshots* to date each of her poems illustrates her recognition that she was "finished with the idea of a poem as a single, encapsulated event, a work of art complete in itself" (BBP 180). Instead, Rich felt that she "needed to indicate to readers [her] sense of being engaged in a long, continuing process," which represented for her "a rejection of the dominant critical idea that the poem's text should be read as separate from the poet's everyday life in the world. It was a declaration that placed poetry in a historical continuity, not above or outside history" (BBP 180).

The title poem of *Snapshots,* which took Rich two years to write, sheds further light on her quest for an autonomous identity. The poem explores representations of a number of different women, among them a "belle in Shreveport," a housewife "Banging the coffee-pot in the sink," a woman poet in the shape of Emily Dickinson drawn away from her writing and "dusting everything on the whatnot every day of life," as well as women working to preserve their fading beauty as they shave their legs "until they gleam" (CEP 145–46). Rich placed these women in varying cultural contexts as she purposefully added quotations that reveal the expectations of the society and time periods these various women inhabit. According to Rich, the poem emerged in the late 1950s as she "was able to write, for the first time, directly about experiencing myself as a woman. The poem was jotted in fragments during children's naps, brief hours in a library, or at 3:00 A.M. after rising with a wakeful child" (LSS

44). The result was a poem written in a "longer looser mode than [she'd] ever trusted [her]self with before" (LSS 44). Since she realized that she had expended a great deal of effort trying "*not* to identify [her]self as a female poet," the poem stands as the first solid indication of Rich's women-centered subject matter that would resound throughout her future work (LSS 44).

The poem presents snapshots of women that question the expectations structuring women's lives. For example, section 4 describes the actions of a housewife who is also a writer. As the housewife sits "Reading while waiting / for the iron to heat," she thinks about Emily Dickinson "writing, *My Life had stood—a Loaded Gun—* / in that Amherst pantry" (CEP 146). The housewife imagined in this section of the poem rarely finds time for herself. Reading and writing become forbidden luxuries in the face of the endless chores expected to be performed each day. Rich purposefully juxtaposed reading with waiting and writing with the pantry, an opposition that Betsy Erkkila, in *The Wicked Sisters: Women Poets, Literary History, and Discord,* believes "stresses the conflict between creative energy and destructive confinement summed up in Dickinson's lines, 'My Life had stood—a Loaded Gun'" (549). Traditionally women had been expected to wait within the confines of the house. While Rich sought safe enclosures in *A Change of World* and *The Diamond Cutters and Other Poems,* the enclosure offered here by the pantry represents a danger to women. As seen in section 2, the housewife described purposefully scalds herself with hot water or holds a match to her thumbnail simply to feel something; however, "nothing hurts her any more," and the trapped position she occupies makes her think, "*Save yourself; others you cannot save*" (CEP 145). There is no solidarity or relief to be found, and confinement brought upon women by societal constraints produces the tensions found in Dickinson's words and Rich's own life experiences.

"Snapshots of a Daughter-in-Law" does more than simply imagine pictures of different women's lives. The poem also questions women's complicity in their locations as victims and objects of beauty and dependency. Rich's speaker accuses the women of failing to work actively against their subjugated positions. For example, section 3 pictures two "thinking" women arguing with one another and states, "The argument [is] *ad feminam,* all the old knives / that have rusted in my back, I drive in yours" (CEP 146). Furthermore section 9, which plays upon a statement by Samuel Johnson regarding women preachers, "*Not that it is done well, but / that it is done at all?,*" questions whether women have played a role in maintaining their own positions of passivity (CEP 148). As Rich writes, "Our blight has been our sinecure: / mere talent was enough for us— / glitter in fragments and rough drafts" (CEP 148). Rich's lines implicate women's complicity in their own oppression.

Unfortunately, for Rich, women seemed content to be thankful for "mere talent" rather than recognizing any effort put forth. In "The Friction of the Mind: The Early Poetry of Adrienne Rich," Mary Slowik accurately summarizes Rich's indictment of women's passivity in this poem: "Even more tragically, women seem to be responsible for their own repression. By quoting male literature and pointing to a larger male world to which women belong, Rich is not denying that men hold women in check. 'Time is male,' she says. But women acquiesce and the poem becomes stronger and stronger in its indictment of women as it goes along. . . . And the speaker herself in sections nine and ten accuses women of refusing to take responsibility for their lives because to live passively and acquiescently is far more comfortable" (154–55). The women in the poem, "bemused by gallantry," fail to break away from the structures confining them; further, the poem suggests that in most cases the women continue to reinforce the very things that entrap them (CEP 148).

More importantly, as the poem presents the complexities of the women's positions, the power of patriarchy becomes more apparent. According to Rich, again in *Of Woman Born,* "Patriarchy is the power of the fathers: a familial-social, ideological, political system in which men—by force, direct pressure, or through ritual, tradition, law, and language, customs, etiquette, education, and the division of labor, determine what part women shall or shall not play, and in which the female is everywhere subsumed under the male. It does not necessarily imply that no woman has power, or that all women in a given culture may not have certain powers" (57). "Snapshots of a Daughter-in-Law" identifies the patriarchal forces playing upon women, while also suggesting the ability of women to transcend those forces. The poem's ending expresses this survival as the speaker envisions a woman, "long about her coming, who must be / more merciless to herself than history" (CEP 149).

Notably, the speaker uses the personal pronoun "I" for the first time in the poem in the closing stanza: "I see her plunge / breasted and glancing through the currents" (CEP 149). This woman, beautiful and moving like a helicopter, brings a cargo that held "no promise then" but once delivered is now "palpable / ours" (CEP 149). As Rich notes in the essay "When We Dead Awaken: Writing as Re-Vision," the poem was "an extraordinary relief" to write (LSS 45). Further, she uses the word "ours"—a signal to women that they too have their own histories and communities that they must reclaim by breaking the confines of patriarchal expectations. In retrospect Rich found the poem "too literal, too dependent on allusion" (LSS 45). She also notes that she "hadn't found the courage yet to do without authorities, or even to use the pronoun 'I'—the woman in the poem is always 'she'" (LSS 45). However, the insertion of "I" in the final stanza in the shape of an observer suggests Rich's developing integration of her life into her work. Further, the comments on women's history point to Rich's willingness to enter the public eye as a spokesperson for women's issues and rights—work she took on in the late 1960s and throughout the 1970s.

Rich, recognizing her new subject matter, explores her transition in the concluding poem of the collection, "The Roofwalker," which speaks of the risky condition in which she now finds herself. This condition has her entering new territory as she learns to record how personal experiences and a patriarchal culture have shaped and reshaped her poetic identity. Rich, again using the pronoun "I," considers laborers repairing a roof and writes, "I feel like them up there: / exposed, larger than life, / and due to break my neck" (CEP 193). As if she is the one repairing the roof, Rich feels exposed and in danger of losing footing. Breaking out of the tradition in which she was trained causes her to realize the enormity of her choice—she is purposefully stepping out of a secure location created by American culture into an unknown space where she has only her own self for protection.

The poem continues as Rich equates the building of a roof with the building of her own life. As she wonders whether it was worth the "infinite exertion" to build a "roof I can't live under," she questions the "blueprints / closing of gaps, / measurings, calculations" upon which she has built her life (CEP 193). Through this self-exploration, she comes to the realization that "A life I didn't choose / chose me: even / my tools are the wrong ones / for what I have to do" (CEP 193). Although she believes that she does not yet possess the proper tools for her trade as a writer, Rich remains aware that she must still choose a personal and poetic path. The poem's speaker equates herself to a "naked man fleeing / across the roofs" (CEP 193) who could simply be a bystander "sitting in the lamplight" (CEP 193) reading about someone "fleeing across the roofs" (CEP 194). As in "Prospective Immigrants Please Note," the speaker faces the choice to act or not act. Rich's integration of the personal pronoun "I" suggests that with this collection she recognizes her need to act rather than observe if she is to write of her experiences as a woman.

In a 1971 interview, Rich discussed the need to take risks in order to move forward: "You know that for a long time you didn't dare yourself, that it's a slow process. It's like the end of that roof-walker poem where you know that you might have been the person who sat indoors reading the newspaper and watching somebody else risk his neck, and that's very much a part of you too. It would be really nice to be a spectator, sometimes" (Plumly 32–33). "The Roofwalker" makes visible Rich's position as she is split between knowing that she should actively take risks if she is to proceed forward and knowing also that she has spent much of her adult life being an observer. Yet we can understand Rich's conflicted position and her growing knowledge that she must forge her own way. She discusses the influence of her sense of a divided identity in "Vesuvius at Home: The Power of Emily Dickinson." Rich asserts that for "many women the stresses of this splitting have led, in a world so ready to assert our innate passivity and to deny our independence and creativity, to extreme consequences: the mental asylum, self-imposed silence, recurrent depression, suicide, and often severe loneliness" (LSS 175–76).

By 1958 Rich was angry and disillusioned about her life. In a journal entry found in *Of Woman Born,* Rich explains that for "months I've been all a tangle of irritations deepening to anger: bitterness, disillusion with society and with myself; beating out at the world, rejecting out of hand. What, if anything, has been positive?" (28). Fortunately for Rich, she was able to answer her own question: "Perhaps the attempt to remake my life, to save it from mere drift and the passage of time" (OWB 28). With the publication of *Snapshots,* Rich emerged as a stronger, more woman-focused poet. *Snapshots of a Daughter-in-Law* portrays Rich's refusal to allow the feelings of depression, felt so often during the years she created her first two collections and during the eight-year silence she endured as she tended to her roles as mother to three children and wife, to defeat her life and her art. Thus in the time between her first two collections of work and *Snapshots of a Daughter-in-Law,* Rich discovered the strength to direct her life actively. While she experienced the "primal agony" that comes from the conflict "between self-preservation and maternal feelings" (OWB 161), she also became "*a woman giving birth to myself*" (OWB 184).

In "Blood, Bread, and Poetry: The Location of the Poet," Rich discusses the time period surrounding the writing and publication of *Snapshots of a Daughter-In-Law.* According to Rich, "as soon as I published—in 1963— a book of poems which was informed by any conscious sexual politics, I was told, in print, that this work was 'bitter,' 'personal'; that I had sacrificed the sweetly flowing measures of my earlier books for a ragged line and a coarsened voice" (BBP 180). While Rich admits that it took time for her not to hear these criticisms, she understood that her writing was changing. As she notes, "I was writing at the beginning of a decade of political revolt and hope and activism. The external conditions for becoming a consciously, self-affirmingly political poet were there, as they had not been when I began to publish a decade earlier" (BBP 180).

The year 1966 brought significant change when the family moved to New York City as her husband joined the faculty at City University of New York. During this time Rich became involved in both the anti-Vietnam movement and the early women's liberation movement. She also began teaching in the City College SEEK Program, a basic writing program for open admissions students. Through these experiences Rich began to feel "more and more urgently the dynamic between poetry as language and poetry as a kind of action, probing, burning, stripping, placing itself in dialogue with others out beyond the individual self" (BBP 181). In turn, as her life became increasingly politicized, her poetry began to change.

The changes did not emerge immediately. Rich's fourth collection, *Necessities of Life,* published in 1966, fails to develop fully the new forms and subject matter that originated in *Snapshots.* Rich said as much in a 1975 interview: "I certainly didn't abandon the new forms I have developed, and I *couldn't* retreat from female themes, but I did retreat from dealing with them as openly as I had in *Snapshots.* And I also became focused on the themes of death, which certainly was not mere coincidence. It was as though something in me was saying, 'If my material, my subject matter as a woman is going to be denied me, there is only *one* other subject for me and that is death.' That's why *Necessities of Life* is a book about death" (Grimstad and Rennie 107). Many of the poems in *Necessities* do explore images and experiences connected to the theme of death. "Breakfast in a Bowling Alley in Utica, New York," for example, speaks of the dying of America's beauty as the land has become overrun with trailers that "put out taproots / of sewage pipe, suckers / of TV aerial" (CEP 217), while other poems detail the dying away of relationships and communication between people. Rich laments in "Like This Together" that "Our words misunderstand us" (CEP 214) and that relationships, like the winter, do not merely die; rather they wear away, "a piece of carrion / picked clean at last, / rained away or burnt dry" (CEP 215). In turn, as the poem "Moth Hour" simply states, "Death, slowly moving among the bleached clouds, / knows us better than we know ourselves" (CEP 246).

However, *Necessities of Life* ultimately refuses to be simply a book about death. Rich's concerns with women's experiences initially raised in *Snapshots of a Daughter-in-Law* do receive attention here, albeit in subtle ways. Rich's careful hand turns to reinterpreting women's lives, observing her family life and position within the family unit, as well as searching for the tools she needs to survive in a male-dominated world. Moreover, poems in the collection outline Rich's growing realization that personal, literary, and national history cannot be separated from the experiences she describes in her work. In *An American Triptych: Anne Bradstreet, Emily Dickinson, Adrienne Rich,* Wendy Martin asserts that with "this collection, Rich articulates her emerging awareness that individual experience cannot be arbitrarily separated from its historic context, and there is a growing conviction that the tension she experiences between her personal values and larger social forms embodies the cultural schism between mind and body, nature and civilization, oppressor and oppressed, which she feels is the basis for patriarchal order" (184). The gap Rich sensed between the life she had been leading as wife and mother and her life as a poet forced her to confront the "cultural schism" between the personal sense of her identity and the social constructions of her identity. Her need to confront the tensions in her life resulted from the desire to feel connected to the world. According to Rich in 1991, "I think that all of that early splitting and fragmentation has made me hungry for connections to be made. Where connections are being made always feels to me like the point of intensest life" (Montenegro 11). In pursuing connections, however, the collection lacks cohesiveness as "each poem seems to stand on its own, a separate stab made by the poet to get at what was bothering her—her own sense of internal fragmentation and the fragmentation or 'splittings,' as she has since called them, in the world around her" (Bennett 198).

The opening, title poem of *Necessities of Life* exposes such a "point of intensest life" and a desire for connection as it suggests a rebirth and shift from a predefined identity to self-definition. The poem's use of the singular pronoun "I" speaks to the focus on identity and a shift from Rich's modernist roots. Beginning as a "small, fixed dot," the poem's speaker presents herself as lacking agency (CEP 205). Rather than taking part in events, the speaker instead sees herself as "pushed into the scene" created "from the pointillist's buzz and bloom" (CEP 205). As the painter's dots begin to "ooze" and "melt," the speaker finds herself influenced by the lives of those she reads about: Jonah, Wittgenstein, and Wollstonecraft. The poem turns as the speaker describes herself as "Scaly as a dry bulb / thrown into a cellar" (CEP 205), and she declares, "I used myself, let nothing use me" as she focuses on the "bare necessities" (CEP 206). Stripped bare, the speaker says she will reenter the world as an eel, suggesting that she will be slippery with an ability to travel to hard-to-reach places.

The final lines of the poem present images of movement from the motion of the eel to mist rising in the air to "old women knitting, breathless / to tell their tales" (CEP 206). The sense of movement correlates to the speaker's growing understanding of identity as a fluid, changing process. In contrast to earlier poems such as "Storm Warnings" and "At a Bach Concert," which present neutral observations, the speaker in this poem actively changes, thus demonstrating how her identity shifts. From the start of the poem, as a child, directed where to go and which experience to take part in, the speaker turns to biographies and life stories of others in a search for new directions. Further, the old women at the end of the poem represent Rich's own growth in recognizing that women's lives are sources of creative power.

In a preface added to her essay "The Tensions of Anne Bradstreet," first written for a Harvard University Press book on Bradstreet's work in 1966 and later republished in *On Lies, Secrets, and Silence* in 1979, Rich reflects on the essay and the subject matter it does not contain. Specifically, Rich notes that the essay did not address the "tension between creative work and motherhood," nor did it raise questions regarding women's creativity, opportunities, and experiences (LSS 21). Rich acknowledges that she wrote out of the "limitations of a point of view which took masculine history and literature at its center" and "which tried from that perspective to view a woman's life and work" (LSS 21). Further, Rich writes, "If such questions were unavailable to me in 1966, it was partly because of the silence surrounding the lives of women—not only our creative work, but the very terms on which that work has been created; and partly for lack of any intellectual community which would take those questions seriously" (LSS 22). In "Necessities of Life," Rich not only forefronts the need for active agency in one's life but also points to her "growing awareness that being a woman is an essential aspect of her unique creative power. Thus we see the significance of the poet's adoption of a female persona who shapes language by choosing her own signs, naming her own names" (Keyes 77).

As the need to address women's experiences develops, *Necessities of Life* also raises, for the first time, Rich's developing concerns with her personal location in North America and the need to understand one's historical context. In the poem "Breakfast in a Bowling Alley in Utica, New York," Rich depicts a piece of life in North America, a place where the song "THIS LAND / IS MY LAND" sobs from the walls and "sounds / mummified" (CEP 216). The question "Is this land her land?," though not explicitly stated, echoes throughout the poem as she chews meat and bread, a traditional North American meal. Within the poem wheat fields, plains, buffalo, trailers, slaughterhouses, sewage pipes, and TV aerials stand as images of life in North America, a life from which the speaker appears removed. At the same time, it is a life "stuck fast by choice" as people struggle to lay down taproots with trailers, an image of mobility and impermanence (CEP 216).

The poem's depiction of small-town North America, with trapped lives and impermanent homes struggling to grow roots, reflects Rich's growing concern with the influence of location. Rich uses the pronoun "I" only once, indicating the speaker's lack of connection within the country she occupies. North American life proceeds around her as she sits at the sandwich counter, but she cannot hear clearly the words "THIS LAND / IS MY LAND" because North America has yet to become her land. The structures created by the laws of the fathers have distanced the speaker from the lives described in the poem. The lack of connection correlates to Rich's own subject position at the time. The woman who came to adulthood in 1950s North America had yet to find her own identity in that country. In the act of looking backward from 1984, Rich explains her predicament in the essay "Blood, Bread, and Poetry: The Location of the Poet": "But at the middle of the fifties I had no very clear idea of my positioning in the world or even that such an idea was an important resources for a writer to have. I knew that marriage and motherhood, experiences which were supposed to be truly womanly, often left me feeling unfit, disempowered, adrift" (BBP 175). In the 1960s Rich moved away from the disempowerment caused by expected gender roles to new poems examining her identity on terms of her own making.

This poetic shift was driven by a conscious resistance to her formalist training. According to Rich, "I did begin to resist the apparent splitting of poet from woman, thinker from woman, and to write what I feared was political poetry. And in this I had very little encouragement from the literary people I knew, but I did find courage and vindication in words like Baldwin's: 'Any real change implies the breakup of the world as one has always known it, the loss of all that gave one an identity, the end of safety'" (BBP 176). In choosing to rediscover her identity, in addition to parsing the influences of the literary past and patriarchal laws upon her life, Rich also recognized that she needed to examine her location in North America. The multiple sources of her sense of alienation needed to be broken down.

As the speaker notes in "Breakfast in a Bowling Alley in Utica, New York," North America is a land for the transient and "land glitters / with temporary life" (CEP 216). In the 1983 essay "North American Tunnel Vision," alone and separated from the life of the country, Rich asks, "What happens to the heart of the artist, here in North America? What toll is taken of art when it is separated from the social fabric? How is art curbed, how are we made to feel useless and helpless, in a system which so depends on our alienation?" (BBP 185). She continues: "Alienation—not just from the world of material conditions, of power to make things happen or stop happening. Alienation from our own roots, whatever they are, the memories, dreams, stories, the language, history, the sacred materials of art" (BBP 185). In the mid-1960s the life that Rich sought was neither transient nor temporary. A desire for connections and roots is strongly voiced here, but in the end "Breakfast in a Bowling Alley in Utica, New York" ends with no solutions or images of the life she sought.

Necessities of Life also points to Rich's desire to establish an autonomous self, as seen in the poem "I Am in Danger—Sir—," which draws upon the life of Emily Dickinson. In "Mining the 'Earth-Deposits': Women's History in Adrienne Rich's Poetry" (1984), Marianne Whelchel asserts that the poem "gives a feminist reinterpretation of Emily Dickinson's much misunderstood 'withdrawal' from the world" (53). The poem's opening stanza questions what we really know of Dickinson due to the various interpretations of her life, including Higginson's famous statement that Dickinson was "half-cracked," and what we can gather from the poetry she left behind. The second phase of the poem pictures Dickinson gardening and housekeeping while her "thought pulsed on behind / a forehead battered paper-thin" (CEP 232). The poem establishes the necessity of language as for Dickinson "the word was more / than a symptom— // a condition of being" (CEP 232). When this word was threatened by "spoiled language" singing in her ears of "Perjury," Dickinson chose retreat, which the poem's final stanza captures: "and in your half-cracked way you chose / silence for entertainment, / chose to have it out at last / on your own premises" (CEP 232). The repetition of the word "chose" highlights Dickinson's agency. Further, Erkkila asserts that the poem's focus on Dickinson's choice to withdraw enables Rich to stress "the connection between her decision to stay at home, her determination to have her own will, and her power to create herself and re-create the world, by yoking the three ideas in the final image of the poem: "on your own premises" (166). The poem ultimately presents "Dickinson herself as not driven back, not vanquished like a defeated general; she chose her retreat not out of weakness but out of a conscious decision 'to have it out at last' on *her* terms" (Whelchel 54).

This depiction of Dickinson resonates in Rich's essay "Vesuvius at Home: The Power of Emily Dickinson." There, Rich writes, "I have a notion that genius knows itself; that Dickinson chose her seclusion, knowing she was exceptional and knowing what she needed" (LSS 160). Rich adds about Dickinson, "Given her vocation, she was neither eccentric nor quaint; she was determined to survive, to use her powers, to practice necessary economies" (LSS 160). Rich also connects Dickinson's choice to her own struggles to establish her voice: "The methods, the exclusions, of Emily Dickinson's existence could not have been my own; yet more and more, as a woman poet finding my own methods, I have come to understand her necessities, could have been witness in her defense" (LSS 158). Within this poem the collection *Necessities of Life* begins to capture Rich's own understanding of what she needed on her own "premises."

Written in the 1960s, a time of intense political and social turmoil due to the Vietnam War, the drive for civil rights, the rise of gay rights, and the assassinations of John F. Kennedy, Robert Kennedy, and Martin Luther King, Jr., among other events, Rich's fifth collection, *Leaflets,* moved her poetry into a political realm. The collection is organized in three sections with poems written from 1965 to 1968. The title of the collection suggests that the poems are "leaflets" documenting the social unrest of the 1960s in North America. In particular, the poems "enact another kind of coming to consciousness" as Rich became more politically active and she was "increasingly aware of the violence she was beginning to interpret as institutionalised within patriarchal forms" (Yorke 38–39). Caught up in the ongoing protests against the Vietnam War and the civil rights efforts within the United States, Rich continued to experience feelings of alienation and being "split at the root." Gender and power relations drove Rich to new explorations, as she explained in a 1987 interview:

> I was thinking a lot about something that wasn't being talked about at the time very much. I was thinking about where sexuality belonged in all this. What is the connection between Vietnam and the lovers' bed? If this insane violence is being waged against a very small country by this large and powerful country in which I live, what does that have to do with sexuality and with what's going on between men and women, which I felt also as a struggle even then? I was married. I was trying to define myself in a number of ways. I could fit into the . . . I couldn't find a model for the way I wanted to be, either in relationship with a man or as a woman in the world. So when the women's movement began to crystallize from the Left and the civil rights movement, that was another and certainly one of the most powerful connections for me. (Montenegro 11–12)

Leaflets contains poems that foreshadow Rich's growing desire to define herself, as seen in "Orion," "Abnegation," and the title poem. Rich cites "Orion" as a turning point in her poetry. In "When We Dead Awaken," she writes that "Orion" is a "poem of reconnection with a part of myself I had felt I was losing—the active principle, the energetic imagination, the 'half-brother' whom I projected, as I had for many years, into the constellation Orion" (LSS 45). The poem opens with the speaker commenting on her attraction to Orion, who has long been her "genius," her "cast-iron Viking" and "helmed / lion-heart king in prison" (CEP 283). However, while the relationship has endured, the speaker notes that her view of Orion has shifted in the second stanza as she calls his sword "an oldfashioned thing" and the "last bravado you won't give over" (CEP 283). As the third stanza begins, the speaker notes that "the stars in it are dim / and maybe have stopped burning" (CEP 283), thus indicating a shift in her view of Orion's powerful stance in the sky. But as Keyes notes, while the speaker "has matured in her perception of Orion," her newfound "conscious-ness is not powerful enough, however, to counter her visceral response: 'as I throw back my head to take you in / an old transfusion happens again: / divine astronomy is nothing to it'" (92–93). For the speaker, Orion retains his power, which rests in his ability to attract.

This male power rests directly opposite the realities of the speaker's situation as stanza 4 shifts to the speaker's interior life: "Indoors I bruise and blunder, / break faith, leave ill enough / alone, a dead child born in the dark" (CEP 283). Unlike Orion, the speaker struggles to locate power, to give birth to creativity. This opposition associates creativity with men, while women are relegated to maternal concerns. As the speaker comments, "children are dying my death / and eating crumbs of my life" (CEP 284). Rich's prose speaks to the dilemma she believed women faced. In *Of Woman Born,* she writes, "Patriarchy has told the woman in labor that her suffering was purposive—was *the* purpose of her existence; that the new life she was bringing forth (especially if male) was of value and that her own value depended on bringing it forth" (OWB 159). As Rich explains in "When We Dead Awaken: Writing as Revision": "Now, to be maternally with small children all day in the old way, to be with a man in the old way of marriage, requires a holding-back, a putting-aside of that imaginative activity, and demands instead a kind of conservatism. I want to make it clear that I am *not* saying that in order to write well, or to think well, it is necessary to become unavailable to others, or to become a devouring ego. This has been the myth of the masculine artist and thinker; and I do not accept it. But to be a female human being trying to fulfill traditional female functions in a traditional way *is* in direct conflict with the subversive function of the imagination" (LSS 43). Rich explains the conflict for women further: "The choice still seemed to be between 'love'—womanly, maternal love, altruistic love—a love defined and ruled by the weight of an entire culture; and egotism—a force directed by men into creation, achievement, ambition, often at the expense of others, but justifiably so" (LSS 46).

"Orion" ends with the speaker recognizing that Orion the huntsman takes no pity on her as he takes "for granted" his power (CEP 284). Looking back at Orion with a "starlike eye / shooting its cold and egotistical spear," the speaker concludes, "Breathe deep! No hurt, no pardon / out here in the cold with you / you with your back to the wall" (CEP 284). The poem captures the tensions Rich felt between her identities as a writer and a wife and mother. As Keyes concludes, the poem, "as written in 1965, is a moving display of the experience of woman as creative artist and the subsequent exhilaration and despair she feels. It suggests that along with re-visioning 'love,' Adrienne Rich also needs to call into question her identification, as an artist, with the male principle" (94–95).

Rich's ongoing drive for agency becomes apparent in a poem such as "The Key." As something slips through a drain grating, Rich questions whether or not she actually heard the slight noise: was it "a coin, a signal, a message / from the indistinct / piercing my indistinctness?" (CEP 308). She wonders how long she has "gone round / and round" seeking the key, the answers to her questions (CEP 308). The search for "the clear statement / of something missing. Over and over / it stops me in my tracks" (CEP 308). The poem's tone lacks the anger that originated in *Necessities of Life.* A sense of defeat rises as the speaker wonders if she is "spiritless with foreknown defeat" (CEP 308).

That sense of defeat can be understood in light of a statement Rich makes in "When We Dead Awaken: Writing as Re-Vision": "No male writer has written primarily or even largely for women, or with the sense of women's criticism as a consideration when he chooses his materials, his theme, his language. But to a lesser or greater extent, every woman writer has written for men even when . . . she was supposed to be addressing women" (LSS 37–38). From her adolescence in the 1930s and 1940s to the publication of *Leaflets* in 1969, Rich wrote primarily for men—starting with her father and moving on to the praise of male poets such as Auden and Randall Jarrell, among others. Her subject matter was dictated by male desires and expectations of what a woman was expected to write. Her subject matter was also dictated by the separation that existed between the role of a woman in North American society and the role of the poet. The two remained disparate for Rich as the expectations that had driven her poetry were not part of her experiences. "The Key" concludes with a slight revision of Rich's emotions, and yet the poem still indicates a sense of defeat overtaking her work at this moment in time: "I've covered this ground too often / with this yellow disc"; further, the poem concludes that the spotlight "limits are described / by the whole night" (CEP 309).

In *My Life, a Loaded Gun*, Bennett speculates that the combination of Rich's father's death and the political upheavals taking place in America at the time affected Rich in such a way that "she was no longer able to make a meaningful connection to the past, and her poetry hangs in a curiously suspended temporal void" (198). Bennett cites the poem "In the Evening" as an example of this inability to connect with the past, as the second stanza states that even "The old masters, the old sources, / haven't a clue what we're about, / shivering here in the half-dark 'sixties" (CEP 287). Once again a lack of connection forced Rich into a passive position, leaving her unable to act. Even the old masters who had long served Rich as guides could no longer help her since "so many changes have occurred and are still occurring" (Bennett 199). "The Key" illustrates such a temporal void as Rich slowly burns out, loses fuel and energy, while she lapses into darkness where even a searchlight will not expose the path she must forge. Her rebirth may come only when she learns to address women, to address the splits within her own self, and to find some way in which to reconcile her lack of connection to the world. Addressing the division between writing for men versus writing for women, Rich writes, "If we have come to the point when this balance might begin to change, when women can stop being haunted, not only by 'convention and propriety' but by internalized fears of being and saying themselves, then it is an extraordinary moment for the woman writer—and reader" (LSS 38). Outwardly, Rich understood the steps she must take. However, those steps seemed inconceivable to Rich at this moment in 1967 when "The Key" was completed.

Rich's ongoing sense of alienation as she searched for ways in which to reconcile the splits within herself may be further understood by the poem "Implosions," in which she writes, "I wanted to choose words that even you / would have to be changed by." The poem introduces what would become a key theme for Rich's work: "Only where there is language is there world" ("The Demon Lover," CEP 293). Rich knew that she needed to find some sort of connection to the world. "Implosions" moves beyond "The Key" as Rich questions the power of language:

> Take the word
> of my pulse, loving and ordinary
> Send out your signals, hoist
> your dark scribbled flags
> but take
> my hand (CEP 318)

She expresses a desire to communicate meaningfully with another person. The desire for connection is threatened by stasis, as the speaker's hands are "knotted in the rope" and she "cannot sound the bell" (CEP 318). With hands "frozen to the switch," she cannot "throw it" as the "foot is in the wheel" (CEP 318). In *Naked and Fiery Forms: Modern American Poetry by Women, a New Tradition,* Suzanne Juhasz points out that Rich's poem marks a turning point in her work for "the poet now knows she must do more than describe the loneliness and separation, as she used to do, for its implications are more deadly than she had understood" (19). Lack of connection leads to stasis, and the poem's speaker longs for movement as the poem concludes:

> When it's finished and we're lying
> in a stubble of blistered flowers
> eyes gaping, mouths staring,
> dusted with crushed arterial blues
>
> I'll have done nothing
> even for you? (CEP 318)

"Implosions" ends with a question, as if the speaker can no longer fathom standing passively by as an observer of life's experiences. Moreover the poem suggests the need for language, for words that "even you / would have to be changed by" to make that connection (CEP 318).

In the title poem of *Leaflets,* Rich shifts to new forms in five sections that reveal an innovative type of written line and different approach to her subject matter. Compared to poems in earlier collections, "Leaflets," as Keyes suggests, "appears formless" as "stanzas have been abandoned for clusters of lines" with fragmented sentences and punctuation that "appears, disappears" (101). This is a new poetic form for Rich and a challenge for readers who "expect the poet to do more work for her readers and to create an ordered sensibility. Rich refuses. This refusal is her newborn power" (Keyes 101). With this new line and form, Rich's work becomes more associative and image driven; further, the poem builds upon the desire for connection and the power of language raised in "Implosions."

The poem's first section situates the speaker awake at night gazing at stars, a solitary individual beneath the expanse of the universe. As the speaker's head "clears of sweet smoke / and poison gas," the speaker seeks a "life without caution / the only worth living," and "that self-defense be not / the arm's first motion" (CEP 330). The poem shifts to situating the speaker within larger contexts such as Chekhov's writings on Russian penal colonies, references to the death of Che Guevara in Bolivia, as well as Bolivia's University of Nanterre, where students had named a theater after Guevara. This integration of public history into the poem highlights Rich's growing exploration of personal and public identities coupled with a desire to create change in the world.

This desire for change emerges fully in the fifth section of the poem, which coalesces around the speaker, the "I," addressing the readers, the "you." Using the image of a leaflet, the speaker repeatedly states her desire to connect with those outside herself:

> I want to hand you this
> leaflet streaming with rain or tears
> but the words coming clear
> something you might find crushed into your hand
> after passing a barricade (CEP 333)

The speaker engages the reader in an effort to share information. The speaker continues:

> I want this to reach you
> who told me once that poetry is nothing sacred
> no more sacred that is
> than other things in your life—
> to answer yes, if life is uncorrupted
> no better poetry is wanted. (CEP 333)

Knowing that poetry is as vital to her life as are her other experiences, as wife, mother, and daughter, Rich desires a poetry that communicates, connects, and engages both personal and public experience. The speaker longs for the leaflet to be "in you already" and "merely something / to leave behind" as individuals carry the information forward (CEP 334). As the poem draws to a close, Rich's speaker states, "I am thinking how we can use what we have / to invent what we need" (CEP 334).

Poetry is the tool that Rich identified for making connection, for situating herself in the world. As such, she took on a new power that can be understood through her comments in *What Is Found There: Notebooks on Poetry and Politics:* "When I'm writing poetry, and often when reading it, the voices fade away as the old integrative powers rush together: it's as if the process of poetry itself temporarily releases me into that realm of human power which Marx said is its own end. By 'human power,' he meant the opposite of possessive, exploitive power: the power to engender, to create, to bring forth fuller life" (50). The appetite for destructiveness, aptly illustrated in a poem such as "The Key," where she feels like a "battery going dead," had kept Rich from using her full powers of invention in her poetry. With "Leaflets," Rich's poem challenges the idea of form—that poetry needs a form as she moves to "invent what we need" to address the world. Significantly, the final line moves from the I/you address to "we." The poet and reader merge in the final lines, suggesting Rich's developing vision of the need for people to work together to create social change, which she believes poetry can help enact.

The collection *Leaflets* ends with a third section that includes Rich's first attempt at writing *ghazals,* a poetic form Rich was drawn to when working on translations of the Urdu poet Mirzah Ghalib, who is recognized for his use of the form. The *ghazal* is structured by associated images and contains up to fifteen couplets. Each line is of a similar length, and the couplet pattern often includes references to the poet. Rich explains her turn to the *ghazal* as a poetic form in her notes to the collection: "While the structure and metrics of the classical *ghazal* form used by Ghalib are much stricter than mine, I adhered to his use of a minimum five couplets to a *ghazal*, each couplet being autonomous and independent of the others. The continuity and unity flow from the associations and images playing back and forth among the couplets in any single *ghazal*" (CEP 425). Rich also explains that her "*ghazals* are personal and public, American and twentieth-century" (CEP 426). With the *ghazal* Rich "found a structure that allowed for a highly associative field of images," about which, once she understood how they worked, she "felt instinctively, this is exactly what I need, there is no traditional Western order that I have found that will contain all these materials" (Montenegro 17).

"Ghazal 7/26/68 I" offers a look at Rich's continued search for a poetry that can "invent what we need" as the speaker converses with someone about the struggle to create change. The opening couplet sets the tone: "Last night you wrote on the wall: Revolution is poetry. / Today you needn't write; the wall has tumbled down" (CEP 349). The lines speak to the power of language, yet with the next couplet, the speaker recognizes that revolution is not easily come by when people have been "taught to respect the appearance behind the reality" (CEP 349). In the third couplet, the speaker shifts to internal transformation, feeling that her pair of eyes "imprisoned for years inside my skull / is burning its way outward" (CEP 349). The fourth couplet shifts the poem outward again, as the speaker walks through rubble of the broken sculpture while leaning on a friend and a brother, creating an image of the individual needing others for survival. The poem's final couplet concludes, "All those joinings! and yet we fought so hard to be unique. / Neither alone, nor in anyone's arms, will we end up sleeping" (CEP 349). Neither alone nor together, the poem's speaker recognizes the struggle for both an individual and a communal identity.

Rich's sixth collection, *The Will to Change,* appeared in 1971 and reveals her growing feminist poetics and challenge to patriarchal power that dominates Rich's later work. The collection's epigraph drawn from Charles Olson's poem "The Kingfishers" speaks to the focus of this latest work: "What does not change / is the will to change" (CEP 358). As Keyes outlines, change in this collection "means transformation, not merely of 'something different' but an actual restructuring of the mind—her mind, and subsequently, other minds" (112); further, the collection clearly positions Rich as a political poet since her subject matter delves into current events, history, and personal experiences as she continues to question patriarchal institutions that have impacted women's lives.

The poem "Planetarium" is one of Rich's transitional poems that questions patriarchal power. Composed in free verse, the poem's forty-five lines were prompted by a visit to a planetarium, where Rich read about the work of Caroline Herschel, an astronomer who lived from 1750 to 1848. Herschel, who was the first woman to identify a comet, went unrecognized in her lifetime, while the works of her brother William, also an astronomer, did not. Rich has identified "Planetarium" as a companion to the earlier poem "Orion," but the poem is significantly different as the focus is not on the male symbol but rather on the power of women's creativity and knowledge creation.

The poem opens vividly: "A woman in the shape of a monster / a monster in the shape of a woman / the skies are full of them" (CEP 361). The images of mythical women, the constellations, are set against images of a "real" woman, "among the Clocks and instruments," who in "her 98 years" discovered eight comets as she rode cages raised in the air to study the stars (CEP 361). Strikingly, these "Galaxies of women" are "doing penance for impetuousness," and yet their drive for knowledge persists as they encounter the NOVA with "every impulse of light exploding / from the core / as life flies out of us" (CEP 361). The speaker not only highlights the life-giving energies in the solar system but also underscores the life-giving capacities of women, thus identifying women's power to create.

The poem's tone then shifts as the speaker reflects on the astronomer's act of seeing:

> What we see, we see
> and seeing is changing
>
> the light that shrivels a mountain
> and leaves a man alive
>
> Heartbeat of the pulsar
> heart sweating through my body
>
> The radio impulse
> pouring in from Taurus (CEP 362)

The images of life abound here through the juxtaposition of the pulsing life of the universe and the pulsing heartbeat of the individual. These varying waves of energy from the light impulses to the pulses of the heart to radio transmissions carried on the air equate to Rich's belief in language as a tool to communicate, to create change. The closing lines of the poem suggest how change might occur as the speaker finds herself bombarded by a "direct path of a battery of signals" and yet stands firm. Through eleven rushed lines with random spaces inserted at times, representing the speaker's fragmentation of thoughts and breaking apart of her mind so it can take a new form, the speaker comments,

> I am an instrument in the shape
> of a woman trying to translate pulsations
> into images   for the relief of the body
> and the reconstruction of the mind. (CEP 362)

The poem ends with the speaker's strongly stated desire to transform her thinking. Unlike in "Orion," the claim here is for a "reconstruction of the mind," rather than the taking on of male power. This claim is reinforced by the active subject position the woman speaker takes in the poem. As discussed, the poem opens with the image of "A woman in the shape of a monster." Yet here the poem ends with the image of "an instrument in the shape / of a woman." For Keyes, this "shift in the imagery indicates a reorientation of the poet's mind. Not simply a personal, subjective self, the 'I' in the poem becomes a transmitter of energy" that is generated from both "*the* body and *the* mind" (119). This combination of mind and body is significant as the poem identifies Rich's recognition of the power of her gender, which her later work will develop.

"The Burning of Paper Instead of Children" emerges as a major transitional poem in *The Will to Change*. The poem was written during a time when Rich was a writing instructor with the SEEK program at City College (Montenegro 16). As Rich explains, she was thinking about language and failure—that the students in the SEEK program were "*expected* to fail, they *intended* to fail, and the SEEK program was trying to show that, no, they don't have to fail" (Montenegro 16). Rich further explains that as a teacher she thought about what it meant to fail in a "classroom situation that is rigged entirely against the student, or in which the teacher is too ignorant to teach. Not ignorant of grammar, but ignorant of the students, ignorant of their cultures. So I was thinking very much about *our* failures, the map of *our* failures—we who consider ourselves so possessed of language, so articulate" (Montenegro 16). At the heart of the poem is the power of language to reveal or hide information, to free or oppress individuals, to make sense of our existence.

The poem is composed of five related sections not just with free verse but also with prose sections, a new step in Rich's writing. The imagery of burning, both external and internal, resonates throughout the poem. The poem is grounded with an epigraph from Daniel Berrigan, who was tried in Baltimore for burning draft records: "I was in danger of verbalizing my moral impulses out of existence" (CEP 363). The poem then opens with a prose section as the speaker, whom we increasingly can relate to Rich herself, describes how her neighbor called about their sons who burned a mathematics book in the backyard. The neighbor's emotions are vivid: "The burning of a book," he says, "arouses terrible sensations in me, memories of Hitler; there are few things that upset me so much as the idea of burning a book" (CEP 363). The description of the neighbor's reaction reveals how present events and personal emotions are influenced by historical events.

The speaker's thoughts shift to libraries and what can be found there. In *Adrienne Rich: The Poet and Her Critics*, Craig Werner explains the speaker's shift in focus: "Her ambivalent response stems in part from the dislocation of her neighbor's concern. Bothered by an abstract *idea,* he shows little interest in the boys' hatred of the educational institution or their choice of a math book, itself a symbol of abstract systemization. While she refuses to romanticize the boys' action, Rich perceives a complexity invisible to her neighbor" (65). Rich reflects on her childhood reading of the story of Joan of Arc, a story so compelling that "they take the book away / because I dream of her too often" (CEP 363). For the speaker, the burning of a book is secondary to other burnings such as that of Joan of Arc and even her own; as the speaker states, "I know it hurts to burn" (CEP 363).

The second section turns to the relationship between lovers and intimate communication, "a time of silence / or few words" (CEP 364). As McDaniel points out, the "poet proposes communication through touch" as "physical love allows a 'relief / from this tongue   this slab of limestone / or reinforced concrete'" (McDaniel 319). Yet the lover realizes that language is necessary to communicate: "knowledge of the oppressor / this is the oppressor's language // yet I need it to talk to you" (CEP 364). Here the lover "becomes not himself the 'oppressor,' but only another victim, forced to use the 'oppressor's language' in order to communicate. Language becomes at once the enabler of and the barrier to private communication and love" (Greenwald 99).

The fifth section picks up the need for language as the poem returns to prose form:

> Some of
> the suffering are: it is hard to tell the truth; this is America; I cannot
> touch you now. In America we have only the present tense. I am in
> danger. You are in danger. The burning of a book arouses no sen-
> sation in me. I know it hurts to burn. There are flames of napalm
> in Catonsville, Maryland. I know it hurts to burn. The typewriter
> is overheated, my mouth is burning, I cannot touch you and this is
> the oppressor's language. (CEP 366)

The lines link the burning of books that opened the poem with the burning of the self in the struggle to create change, as well as with the burning of children by napalm in Vietnam, which the poem brings home to Catonsville, Maryland. Further, the poem suggests that the poet, though it "hurts to burn" and the "typewriter is overheated," possesses the ability to work through the oppressor's language to find new ways to communicate, a message that would become a core element of Rich's future writings.

CHAPTER 3

Feminist Poetics

As the 1970s unfolded, Adrienne Rich's poetry turned fully to feminist concerns of gender, sexuality, and women's history as well as a continued interest in the power of language. In the foreword to *On Lies, Secrets, and Silence,* Rich outlines how women's history has "been muffled in silence over and over" and "women's work and thinking has [*sic*] been made to seem sporadic, errant, orphaned of any tradition of its own" (LSS 11). Rich argues that women's culture, however, is and has always been active: "women have been the truly active people in all cultures, without whom human society would long ago have perished, though our activity has most often been on behalf of men and children. Today women are talking to each other, recovering an oral culture, telling our life-stories, reading aloud to one another books that have moved and healed us, analyzing the language that has lied about us, reading our own words aloud to each other" (LSS 13).

Rich's work produced during this time period reflects her belief that women need to take action to counter patriarchal institutions and that such action can be fueled by lesbian/feminism: "It is also crucial that we understand lesbian/feminism in the deepest, most radical sense: as that love for ourselves and other women, that commitment of the freedom of all of us, which transcends the category of 'sexual preference' and the issue of civil rights, to become a politics of *asking women's questions,* demanding a world in which the integrity of all women—not a chosen few—shall be honored and validated in every aspect of culture" (LSS 17). Further, Rich was inspired by increasing signs of women's awakening consciousness: "The argument will go on whether an oppressive economic class system is responsible for the oppressive nature of male/female relations, or whether, in fact, patriarchy—the domination of males—is the original model of oppression on which all others are based. But in the last few years the women's movement has drawn inescapable and illuminating connections between our sexual lives and our political institutions. The sleepwalkers are coming awake, and for the first time this awakening has a collective reality; it is no longer such a lonely thing to open one's eyes" (LSS 35). Within this context of the burgeoning women's movement, Rich's poetry turned overtly political, a change that had been long in coming. In "Blood, Bread, and Poetry: The Location of the Poet" (1984), Rich reflects on her poetic development: "Even before I called myself a feminist or a lesbian, I felt driven—for my own sanity—to bring together in my poems the political world 'out there'—the world of children dynamited or napalmed, of the urban ghetto and militarist violence, and the supposedly private, lyrical world of sex and of male/female relationships" (BBP 181).

Rich also recounts how the social contexts of the late 1960s and 1970s were changing her life and the lives of other women: "Women were now talking of domination, not just in terms of economic exploitation, militarism, colonialism, imperialism, but within the family, in marriage, in child rearing, in the heterosexual act itself. . . . We began naming and acting on issues we had been told were trivial, unworthy of mention: rape by husbands or lovers; the boss's hand groping the employee's breast; the woman beaten in her home with no place to go; the woman sterilized when she sought an abortion; the lesbian penalized for her private life by loss of her child, her lease, her job" (BBP 182). This new subject matter entered Rich's poems as she increasingly distanced herself from the male formalist tradition, resulting in the two groundbreaking collections published in the 1970s, *Diving into the Wreck* (1973) and *The Dream of a Common Language* (1978), along with *The Will to Change* in 1971, that articulate Rich's developing vision of women's history, community, and identity.

Rich's seventh collection, *Diving into the Wreck,* received the National Book Award. It also announced a new feminist vision to Rich's poetry and "established Rich as a major voice in the women's movement" (Werner, *Poet and Her Critics,* 9). In *The Dream and the Dialogue,* Alice Templeton points out that while many of Rich's early works overtly or covertly handle themes about women's lives, those works do not fit the term "feminist" as well as *Diving into the Wreck* does; she explains that while many of the earlier poems "individually experiment with fragmented forms and challenge the confines of interior lyric consciousness and traditional lyric form, Rich's poetic project is not consistently directed by a feminist vision" (33). Templeton's assertion rings true since much of Rich's earlier work depends on an acceptance of and then an ambivalence toward the rules and expectations of the literary past she was trained to follow as a child and young adult. Furthermore, Rich's attempt to stick to objectivity in her poetry prevented her from delving into the patriarchal values that structured her life.

However, with *Diving into the Wreck* a major change takes place as Rich allows her anger regarding male domination to take shape in the body of her poems and directly challenge what she views as "A man's world. But finished" ("Waking in the Dark," DW 8). As she does so, Rich represents the grow-ing women's movement in the 1970s as she spends the collection exploring women's developing consciousness and recovery of their histories. In a review of *Diving into the Wreck,* Margaret Atwood states that it is a "book of explo-rations, of travels. The wreck she is diving into, in the very strong title poem, is the wreck of obsolete myths, particularly myths about men and women" (280). Further, Atwood explains, "This quest—the quest for something beyond myths, for the truths about men and women, about the 'I' and the 'You,' the He and the She, or more generally (in the references to wars and persecutions of various kinds) about the powerless and the powerful—is presented throughout the book through a sharp, clear style and through metaphors which become their own myths" (281).

Challenges to patriarchy and male history take place throughout the collec-tion as seen in the poem "When We Dead Awaken," a companion to the essay of the same title written in 1971 and subsequently published in *On Lies, Secrets, and Silence.* The poem expresses the need for women's history and women's community, which is captured in the first section of the poem as Rich's speaker sits with another woman knitting as they work "to remake / this trailing knitted thing, this cloth of darkness, / this woman's garment, trying to save the skein" (DW 5). This act of knitting attempts to "remake" the literal tangled yarn but also the metaphorical "cloth of darkness" that represents women's history. Such remaking calls to mind Rich's discussion of the act of "re-vision" in the poem's companion essay and her belief that women must re-vision history. For Rich, this act of re-vision is a political act of necessity: "Re-vision—the act of looking back, of seeing with fresh eyes, of entering an old text from a new criti-cal direction—is for women more than a chapter in cultural history: it is an act of survival" (LSS 35). Survival may take place in women coming together as the image of knitting, an activity traditionally associated with women, "suggest[s] that women must recreate [*sic*] themselves, using their traditional power (for example, by valuing female art forms) and perhaps a new power—female bond-ing" (Keyes 145–46).

The poem "Incipience" suggests that women's new power is just waiting to begin; however, this new beginning remains just beyond reach, for change takes place "by inches" as Rich's speaker documents her life "hour by hour, word by word," longing to imagine the "existence / of something uncreated / this poem / our lives" (DW 11). The poem juxtaposes the desire for something new with the image of a man dreaming of women who "have the heads and breasts of women / the bodies of birds of prey" and who also "turn into silver serpents" as he replicates the images that have trapped women (DW 11). The poem concludes with the women moving outside the "frame of his dream" as they "are stumbling up the hill / hand in hand, stumbling and guiding each other / over the scarred volcanic rock" (DW 12). If the women are to survive, if (re)visioning is to take place, the poem suggests that the women must step outside the frame of male history, lean on one another, and step into the scarred world.

Yet Rich still struggles against a social order that is "too numb to get the message / in a world masculinity made / unfit for women or men" ("Merced," DW 36). To confront this world, Rich turns to androgyny as a possible solution in the title poem "Diving into the Wreck." With androgyny, Rich suggests a potential pathway to connecting the oppositions that exist between the two sexes. The poem rests on an extended metaphor of diving and a quest for knowledge. After first consulting "the book of myths" for guidance and then loading her tools, a camera and a knife, Rich's speaker puts on a dive suit and enters the deep. The inclusion of the knife suggests that the mission is a search for knowledge that may be dangerous as Rich's speaker moves to "explore / the wreck and not the story of the wreck / the thing itself and not the myth" (DW 23).

The poem shifts on the diver's transformation once the wreck is reached. There the diver takes on both masculine and feminine qualities, becoming both the "mermaid" and the "merman," a merging represented by a shift to the first-person-plural voice of "we" (DW 24). The poem's dual speaker dives into the hold declaring, "I am she: I am he" (DW 24). The androgyne confronts the wreck only to discover cargo "left to rot" (DW 24). The androgyne compares him/herself to the "half-destroyed instruments / that once held to a course / the water-eaten log / the fouled compass" (DW 24). The tools for navigating distances are worn away, suggesting that the distances between men and women may be similarly difficult to traverse. Further, the poem's final lines indicate that the merger for women may be dangerous as the diver carries "a book of myths / in which / our names do not appear" (DW 24).

Rich, on the original cover from the first printing of *Diving into the Wreck*, offered the following statements about the collection: "A coming-home to the darkest and richest sources of my poetry: sex, sexuality, sexual wounds, sexual identity, sexual politics: many names for pieces of one whole. I feel this book continues the work I've been trying to do—breaking down the artificial barriers between private and public, between Vietnam and the lovers' bed, between the deepest images we carry out of our dreams and the most daylight events

'out in the world.' This is the intention and longing behind everything I write"
(Keyes 133). This longing for a breaking down of barriers comes in the shape of
the androgyne—the being who could encompass both poet and wife, poet and
mother, poet and the son her father wished he had. Yet in 1973 the androgyne
offered only a temporary solution and connection of the public and private,
poet and woman, for Rich. In her next collection, Rich states in the poem
"Natural Resources," "There are words I cannot choose again: / *humanism
androgyny*" (DCL 66). Importantly, though, Rich's realization of the failure of
androgyny to create the freedom she desired led to the transformational poetry
that emerged in 1978 in the collection *The Dream of a Common Language.*

The Dream of a Common Language contains three sections: "Power";
"Twenty-One Love Poems"; and "Not Somewhere Else but Here." The first section delves into the sources of women's power; the second section explores love
between women in a sequence of love poems; and the closing section situates
Rich fully in her social context, within history. The collection also continues
themes from *Diving into the Wreck,* particularly the drive for women's community, history, and agency.

The collection opens with the often-anthologized poem "Power," which
celebrates the life of Marie Curie. The narrator, "reading about Marie Curie,"
speculates,

> she must have known she suffered   from radiation sickness
> her body bombarded for years   by the element
> she had purified (DCL 3)

The poem concludes,

> She died   a famous woman   denying
> her wounds
> denying
> her wounds   came   from the same source as her power (DCL 3)

This source of power metaphorically can be read as Curie's grasping of the
male-dominated field of science as she led the field in researching radioactivity.
Here, Curie's gender claims traditional male powers of creation and discovery.
Yet the poem's paradox lies in the fact that Curie's very power, her discovery of
radium, also killed her. Thus the collection opens acknowledging that women's
search for power is neither simple nor carefree.

The second poem in the collection, "Phantasia for Elvira Shatayev," continues the focus on power and suggests that perhaps women's power can come
from women's community. In August 1974 a Russian women's climbing team
attempted to ascend Lenin Peak, the third highest mountain in the Soviet

Union. The women encountered a storm, and all perished. While the Russian press did not report on the event, three articles written by an American climber, Christopher Wren, came out in the *New York Times* (Bell 90). Relying on these accounts, Rich's poem envisions the women's journey in three sections, the first of which details the women's death in the storm and how they found strength, the second of which relates Shatayev's husband's recovery of and burying of the bodies, and the last of which contains Rich's polemical call for women to gain power through communal actions.

The first section allows us to hear the voice of Elvira Shatayev, already dead, as she recounts what happened to the group of women when the storm hit. Immediately the reader senses the drive for community among women present in the poem as Shatayev says, "If in this sleep I speak / it's with a voice no longer personal / (I want to say *with voices*)" (DCL 4). The line sectioned off in parentheses reveals Rich's own desire for a bond between women. Rich believed that that connection would enable women to overcome the societal powers that entrapped them and kept them dependent on men; such an escape from dependence would ensure women's survival as a group. Furthermore, according to Bennett, women's acceptance of one another found through a common bond would enable women "to cease to be objects in their own eyes and in the eyes of others and [they will] become fully themselves" (230).

The poem further details what the women gained from coming together as a group as Shatayev's husband approaches their frozen bodies and prepares to bury them. Elvira Shatayev comments on his approach, "You climbed here for yourself / we climbed for ourselves" (DCL 5). She knows he came here to resolve his individual pain and suffering. The women, on the other hand, climbed for themselves as a group in order to ease their own suffering and pain through a common goal and effort for independence. Thus the women's story, according to Rich, never ends in the way the husband's story will. Once the husband has eased his pain, performed the burial, and told his story, the women's story "does not end" as they "stream / into the unfinished the unbegun / the possible" (DCL 5). Finding life and an energy source in one another, the women transcend their own deaths and live on. Their choice to attempt the climb and their subsequent deaths mean nothing in the face of what they found together through their common experience.

The women's lives are sustained physically; as Elvira Shatayev explains, after the women's deaths, the mountain itself has taken on the "imprint of our minds / through changes elemental and minute / as those we underwent / to bring each other here" (DCL 5). Further, the women's lives are sustained by the lives of other women. Shatayev asserts that in "choosing ourselves each other and this life," the women's efforts continue as they are "somewhere still enacted and continuing" (DCL 5). The poem offers an alternative to patriarchal culture by celebrating women's community and the search for self-knowledge. This drive for self-knowledge, in particular, is essential work. Rich explains, "Until we can understand the assumptions in which we are drenched we cannot know ourselves. And this drive to self-knowledge, for women, is more than a search for identity: it is part of our refusal of the self-destructiveness of male-dominated society" (LSS 35). According to the voice of Shatayev at the start of the poem, each woman had felt herself seeking self-knowledge for a long time: "For months for years each one of us / had felt her own *yes* growing in her / slowly forming" (DCL 4). The women found power through their collective endeavor and newfound strength.

These women attempted to climb a mountain in order to prove to themselves their own strengths as women. As the poem recounts, they chose a community of women and found a source of energy in each other that continues beyond death. The conclusion of the poem reinforces the importance of community, noting that "we have always been in danger / down in our separateness," but through their mutual experience, they have "touched our strength" (DCL 6). The poem closes,

> *What does love mean*
> *what does it mean   "to survive"*
> *A cable of blue fire ropes our bodies*
> *burning together in the snow. We will not live*
> *to settle for less   We have dreamed of this*
> *all of our lives.* (DCL 6)

The danger of the storm that ultimately overcame the women proves to be a gift since through that danger the women drew upon each other for strength. Furthermore the poem brings up the question of what type of survival women desire and indicates that the women who died found a community with each other; a source of energy and life through a "cable of blue fire" is preferable. However, while the vision of a women's community here is inspiring, it is also important to note that the climbing team's self-determination and self-empowerment, like Marie Curie's pursuit of knowledge, came at great cost—their lives. Yet, Rich's belief that the "awakening of consciousness is not like the crossing of a frontier—one step and you are in another country" underlies the poem (LSS 48). Women's independence and community will not come without losses or pain.

Other poems in *The Dream of a Common Language* attend to the issue of creating a new language, "The drive / to connect. The dream of a common language," that would forge connection between people, thus continuing an ongoing concern in Rich's work ("Origins and History of Consciousness," DCL 7). Rich's dialogue with language is most apparent in "Cartographies of Silence," in which she details a map of silences created by the oppressor's language and laws, yet finds herself returning to words, realizing that she needs the oppressor's language to create change, reminiscent of the earlier poem "Leaflets." The opening section questions whether a common language exists, noting that a conversation "begins / with a lie"; that "A poem can begin / with a lie. And be torn up" (DCL 16). Conversations have "other laws" that create "false energy" and alienation (DCL 16). Rich juxtaposes this lack of communication with the endless repetition of a woman's life—the music that plays "hour upon hour in the apartment"; the repeated answering of the telephone; the use of "the old script over and over" (DCL 16). Caught in this cycle of passivity, Rich's speaker identifies the "loneliness of the liar / living in the formal network of the lie // twisting the dials to drown the terror / beneath the unsaid word" (DCL 17).

The poem implies the complicit role women play in perpetuating ongoing relationships and power structures that control them. In repeating an "old script over and over," women find themselves trapped, "living in the formal network of the lie" (DCL 16–17). The poem implicitly challenges this passive position, suggesting the need for women to break out of the patterns that guide their interactions. It cannot be unconsciously that Rich employed the phrase "unsaid word," which brings to mind the poem "An Unsaid Word" from her first collection, A Change of World. "An Unsaid Word" illustrates the socially created and still-believed position women in the 1950s were expected to occupy and fulfill willingly:

> She who has power to call her man
> From that estranged intensity
> Where his mind forages alone,
> Yet keeps her peace and leaves him free,
> And when his thoughts to her return
> Stands where he left her, still his own,
> Knows this the hardest thing to learn. (CEP 28)

The woman in the poem finds herself trapped in a marriage and unable to speak out or influence her husband. She has learned that silence coupled with a consistent, unchanging presence meets her husband's expectations.

Yet such a world, as section 2 of "Cartographies of Silence" indicates, is filled with loneliness and fear drawn from a life that prevents choices and an independent identity. Women's silence ensures that they are unable to ask questions. A limiting situation develops for women as they seek words to make change in a world where they have been denied both words and power. The routine of their lives and the expectations so carefully laid out for women have created a "technology of silence" guided by "rituals, etiquette / the blurring of terms" (DCL 17). Rich's speaker notes that silence itself "can be a plan" that creates a "blueprint to a life" with a "presence," "history," and "form" (DCL 17). Silent acceptance of the constructs of a life being wife, mother, daughter-in-law, among others, thrusts women into predefined roles with little or no room for self-knowledge.

"Cartographies of Silence" explores other dangers associated with silence. Silence has historically aided in establishing the constructs of women's identities. However, according to Joanne Feit Diehl's "Cartographies of Silence: Rich's *Common Language* and the Woman Poet," silence benefits women and prevents them from "echoing or antithetically mimicking the patriarchal voice" (102); further, "the power of silence [also] potentially casts a shadow, for the very refusal to speak may not be a simple desire to escape the structures of conventional discourse, but may, in the absence of any interpretative gesture, signify the negative act of willful withholding" (102). Rich found herself in a bind; she could remain silent, thus protecting herself from indulging in and perpetuating patriarchal discourse, and yet in doing so she ran the risk of being viewed as keeping her opinions to herself. The idea of willfully withholding one's words creates more danger than the unintentional, almost unavoidable, use of patriarchal words, for by remaining silent, Rich may actively have reinforced the identities that oppress women in society.

Yet, Rich recognized the bind in which she and other women found themselves after being ruled for so long by a language and society that preestablished their identities. Rich's speaker comments, "It was an old theme even for me: / Language cannot do everything" (DCL 19). For language to do everything—to solve the schisms between mind and culture, oppressor and oppressed, husband and wife, woman and poet—was what Rich desired and yet may not be possible. The poem concludes, however, reinforcing the potential power of language to forge connection, the need to continue choosing language: "what in fact I keep choosing // are these words, these whispers, conversations / from which time after time the truth breaks moist and green" (DCL 20).

The centerpiece of *The Dream of a Common Language* is Rich's "Twenty-One Love Poems." These poems stand out as the strongest statement of Rich's newly forming lesbian-identified vision in their powerful evocation of a relationship between two women. In "Disloyal to Civilization: The *Twenty-One Love Poems* of Adrienne Rich," Adrian Oktenberg explains that these poems "are *feminist* in that they are woman-identified; they acknowledge, define and explore one set of the possibilities of love between women; they recognize the connection, the primary bond, between women as a source of integrity and strength. They are also *radically* feminist in that they constitute a critique, a re-vision, of patriarchal notions of love" (342).

The fifteenth poem of the poetic sequence ends with lines that may be viewed as the central fact surrounding *The Dream of a Common Language,* and it also stands as another sign of why the collection was such a pivotal turning point in Rich's career: "Only she who says / she did not choose, is the loser in the end" (DCL 33). In this collection Rich more visibly takes control of her experiences as she acknowledges that the act of *not* choosing keeps her and other women trapped by societal rules and, even more dangerous, complicit in their own entrapment. In "Twenty-One Love Poems," Rich consciously chooses lesbianism and women-identified communities as her new path. Motivated by both the women's movement of the 1970s and her own desire for relationships with women, Rich's active choice enabled her to grapple with her misgivings about and dislike of the patriarchal order. Her choice also enabled her to confront an opposition that had existed since her birth—that of, to use Rich's own terms, the tensions between a compulsory heterosexuality and a lesbian continuum.

It is important to note that the term "lesbian continuum" is not simply about sexual orientation. According to Rich in her 1980 essay "Compulsory Heterosexuality and Lesbian Existence," "I mean the term *lesbian continuum* to include a range—through each woman's life and throughout history—of woman-identified experience, not simply the fact that a woman has had or consciously desired genital sexual experience with another woman" (BBP 51). In "Adrienne Rich and Lesbian/Feminist Poetry," Catherine Stimpson argues that "lesbianism forms a 'continuum,' a range of 'woman-identified' activities that embraces eros, friendship and intensity between women, resistance to gynephobia, and female strength" (255). Through this continuum Rich forges a path to re-vision women's experiences. For too long, as Rich writes in poem I of "Twenty-One Love Poems," women have existed amid images of women created by male experiences, values, and viewpoints. "No one has imagined us," Rich's speaker states (DCL 25). The poem asserts that women "want to live like trees, / sycamores blazing through the sulfuric air," and yet the reality is that women remain marked by stereotypes as seen in poem IV (DCL 25). There, Rich's speaker tells us her experience as, loaded down with groceries, she makes a dash for an elevator:

> I dash for the elevator
> where a man, taut, elderly, carefully composed

lets the door almost close on me.—*For God's sake hold it!*
I croak at him.—*Hysterical*,—he breathes my way. (DCL 26)

The speaker's experience plays out the assumptions that have plagued women as the elderly man, carefully composed, perpetuates existing stereotypes of women as "hysterical."

Continuing a theme begun in "Cartographies of Silence," poem V examines women's silence; however, this time the silence is due to women being shut off from literature and creativity. While Kenneth, a person in the poem, lines up books by Blake and Kafka to look at while he writes, Rich suggests that such books hold no place for women, nor do they inspire women to creativity for they sustain passive, stereotypical images of women: Jonathan Swift's "loathing the women's flesh while praising her mind"; Johann Wolfgang von Goethe's "dread of the Mothers"; ghosts of "artists dying in childbirth; "wise-women charred at the stake" (DCL 27). Rich's speaker imagines the "centuries of books unwritten" as women could not "speak / to our life" (DCL 27).

The poem asserts that women have been kept from literature and writing since they have been silenced, burned at the stake, or simply did not have the time outside of their duties as wives, mothers, and daughters to sit down and compose. In "Compulsory Heterosexuality and Lesbian Existence," Rich lists the characteristics of male power, which includes "*the power of men*" (BBP 36) that works "to cramp [women's] creativeness" (BBP 38). Drawing upon the words of Mary Daly, Rich asserts that culture defines "male pursuits as more valuable than female within any culture, so that cultural values become the embodiment of male subjectivity, restriction of female self-fulfillment to marriage and motherhood; sexual exploitation of women by male artists and teachers; the social and economic disruption of women's creative aspirations; erasure of female tradition" (BBP 38). Women's silence, pervasively enforced by male power, creates inequality and leaves women with no literary history of their own. With no role models to call upon, for Rich, the world is only half a world. As she writes in poem IX, "I fear this silence / this inarticulate life" (DCL 29).

The seventh poem continues the sequence's reflection on the act of writing, recognizing that without care the poet's works can replicate images of women in history; as Rich's speaker thinks about her lover in poem VII, "when away from you I try to create you in words, / am I simply using you, like a river or a war?" (DCL 28). Further, the poet questions if she has participated in the "failure to want our freedom passionately enough" so that "blighted elms, sick rivers, massacres would seem / mere emblems of that desecration of ourselves?" (DCL 28). Rich's lines push the poet to be responsible for a poem's images and to create a poem that accurately represents women's lives. Here, as Templeton asserts, "the poet does not want to 'use' her lover or exploit materials for poetry—she wants to create poetry that serves rather than manipulates us. In this regard she questions her own motives as a poet and affirms the power of poetry to reveal our own complicity in the 'desecration' of ourselves and the world" (*Dream and the Dialogue*, 86).

At the same time, "Twenty-One Love Poems" presents love between two women and takes on the sexualized body, a site of contestation and politics as Rich writes in "Notes toward a Politics of Location": "The politics of pregnability and motherhood. The politics of orgasm. The politics of rape and incest, of abortion, birth control, forcible sterilization. Of prostitution and marital sex. Of what had been named sexual liberation. Of prescriptive heterosexuality. Of lesbian existence" (BBP 212–13). "Twenty-One Love Poems" represents Rich's newly formed lesbian-identified vision that developed in the 1970s through the work's powerful evocation of a relationship between two women as well as the suggestion of the power to be found in women's community. In *Reconstituting the World*, Judith McDaniel writes, "in these poems Rich shows us a glimpse of the power generated by love, specifically the love of women for women," with the poems' strength resting "in the discovery of the self in another, the range of knowing and identification that seems most possible in same-sex love" (320).

Oktenberg explains that most of the "action of the 'Poems' describes the process of trial and error by which the lovers must explore their love. Conventional love, as patriarchy would have them experience it, is useless" (336). In doing so, the poems take on a civilization that "has shaped our consciousness of love, and therefore our experience of it, into gynephobic, patriarchal forms" (Oktenberg 342). The poems articulate the difficulty of two women coming together, striving to "move openly together / in the pull of gravity, which is not simple" (II, DCL 25). As the two lovers are middle-aged, they must make up for lost time, while also recognizing that "each of us will help the other live, / and somewhere, each of us will help the other die" (III, DCL 26). The women lack a guide for shaping their relationship—"whatever we do together is pure invention" (XIII, DCL 31)—as they do not fit into society's belief in "heterosexuality as *the* natural emotional and sensual inclination for women" (BBP 56).

We see the lesbian body emerge most clearly in "The Floating Poem, Unnumbered," which appears in the middle of the love poem sequence. This poem, one of the most sexualized in Rich's body of work at that time, captures the intimacy of the women's passion as well as the self-affirmation the narrator finds in the relationship. The narrator comments,

> Whatever happens with us, your body
> will haunt mine—tender, delicate
> your lovemaking, like the half-curled frond
> of the fiddlehead fern in forests
> just washed by sun. (DCL 32)

Relishing the "innocence and wisdom of the place my tongue has found," the narrator feels the other woman's "touch" on her body as "firm, protective, searching / me out, your strong tongue and slender fingers / reaching where I had been waiting years for you / in my rose-wet cave" (DCL 32). In "Blue Ghazals" from *The Will to Change,* Rich writes, *"The moment when a feeling enters the body* / is political. This touch is political" (CEP 372). This vivid imagery, the intimate touch between the two women, situates the lesbian body as a politicized location, one with external and internal forces impacting the women's relationship as described in poem XVII: "this we were, this is how we tried to love, / and these are the forces they had ranged against us, / and these are the forces we had ranged within us, / within us and against us, against us and within us" (DCL 34).

However, the forces within and outside the women become too much to withstand. As the sequence begins to draw to a close in poem XX, the other lover is "drowning in secrets" with "fear wound round her throat / and choking her like hair" (DCL 35), which separates the pair. In poem 21 Rich's speaker ends the sequence alone, but the poem suggests that the intimacy found between the two women is a site of power and self-definition as the speaker forcefully notes her new, consciously chosen position:

> I choose to be a figure in that light,
> half-blotted by darkness, something moving
> across that space, the color of stone:
> greeting the moon, yet more than stone:
> a woman. I choose to walk here. And to draw this circle. (DCL 36)

Choosing a lesbian existence and a woman-identified community, Rich found herself actively taking charge of her life, identity, and location in North America. She focused on her identity as a woman, and she acted in the closing poem by choosing to draw the lines that surrounded her. While "Twenty-One Love Poems" seemingly concludes in defeat as the relationship fails and Rich's speaker is alone at the end, it is significant that the work, though modeled on the sonnet form, resists following the formal structure fully. Virginia Frankel Harris explains that Rich's love poems "refuse traditional generic encoding, such as a sonnet's closure as it is exhibited in the Italian question and answer form or in the Shakespearean structure that ends with a conclusive or summarizing couplet" (143). Further, as written in the love poems, the female body lies "outside the parameters of male pleasure," which Harris sees as a re-visioning of male poetic strategies of "closure or objectification" (144). Thus the lesbian body offers Rich a site of resistance to the male gaze, and the sequence itself offers a powerful alternative for women.

The collection's third section, "Not Somewhere Else, but Here," opens up that new civilization with poems written directly for and about women. For example, "Paula Becker to Clare Westhoff" reads as a letter from Becker to Westhoff reflecting on their friendship, subsequent marriages, and desire to pursue their own work as artists. "Sibling Mysteries," dedicated to Rich's sister, considers their relationship as it has become distant through the years. It is with the final poem of the collection, "Transcendental Etude," that Rich hones in again on the power of language, as well as Rich's drive to expand her consciousness. The poem calls for a time when women must make conscious choices. Rich's speaker asserts,

> But there come times—perhaps this is one of them—
> when we have to take ourselves more seriously or die;
> when we have to pull back from the incantations,
> rhythms we've moved to thoughtlessly,
> and disenthrall ourselves, bestow
> ourselves to silence, or a severer listening, cleansed
> of oratory, formulas, choruses, laments, static
> crowding the wires. (DCL 74)

Rich's words here indict language that ritualizes women's experiences, calling for women to break free of oratory and formulas. To break free, Rich's speaker calls on women to "cut the wires" so that they may find themselves in "freefall," untethered like the "rift / in the Great Nebula" (DCL 75). In this freeing space, Rich's speaker notes,

> No one who survives to speak
> new language, has avoided this:
> the cutting-away of an old force that held her
> rooted to an old ground
> the pitch of utter loneliness
> where she herself and all creation
> seem equally dispersed, weightless, her being a cry
> to which no echo comes or can ever come. (DCL 75)

Cutting the wires enables women to uproot and free themselves. While the cutting away of old forces, such as the identity of a housewife or mother, may frighten, it may also empower women to seek self-knowledge and movement. This movement emerges in the later parts of the poem as Rich's speaker senses "a whole new poetry beginning here" (DCL 76). The woman in the poem moves away from the "jargon in the room" to arrange scraps of cloth for a quilt. There the woman brings together mind and body, "pulling the tenets of a life together" with care for the "many-lived, unending / forms in which she finds herself" (DCL 77). These forms range from the "shard of broken glass" that can cut flesh, to a "plentiful, soft leaf" that "soothes the wound," to a "stone foundation, rockshelf further / forming underneath everything that grows" (DCL 77). The forms hold power both to slice and to heal; further, in this new-found position of strength, Rich found herself developing a firm foundation from which to live.

Building upon the feminist vision of *The Dream of a Common Language,* Rich's *A Wild Patience Has Taken Me This Far,* published in 1981, handles a number of ongoing themes. In poems such as "Images," "Rift," and "Mother-in-Law," Rich continues her exploration and indictment of language and the assumptions, both political and personal, that are embedded within language. At the same time she embarks on a rescuing of women's histories in poems such as "Culture and Anarchy"; "For Julia in Nebraska," which discusses Willa Cather; and "Grandmothers." Moreover a third theme regarding self-identity emerges forcefully in many poems, including "Integrity," "Transit," "For Memory," and "The Spirit of Place." What connects all these themes in *A Wild Patience Has Taken Me This Far* is Rich's ability to examine the continual interactions of language, history, and identity.

The theme of self-identity emerges in the third poem in the collection, "Integrity." The poem must have held importance for Rich since she took the title of the collection from the first line of "Integrity" (Keyes 183). An epigraph from Webster's dictionary stands beneath the title and provides a definition: "the quality or state of being complete; unbroken condition; entirety" (WP 8). The definition is interesting in light of Rich's 1982 article "Split at the Root: An Essay on Jewish Identity," which concludes with her wondering if she will ever achieve wholeness and connection, an issue that would emerge full blown in *Your Native Land, Your Life* (1986). Rich writes, "Sometimes I feel I have seen too long from too many disconnected angles: white, Jewish, anti-Semite, racist, anti-racist, once-married, lesbian, middle-class, feminist, exmatriate southerner, *split at the root*—that I will never bring them whole" (BBP 122). Rich believed that the fragments of her identity, which all existed in opposition

to one another, would never be connected. Yet, here in "Integrity," Rich takes a
step toward transforming her perceived weaknesses into sources of strength:

> but really I have nothing but myself
> to go by; nothing
> stands in the realm of pure necessity
> except what my hands can hold.
>
> *Nothing but myself? . . . My selves.*
> After so long, this answer. (WP 8)

Thirty years after the publication of her first collection of verse, Rich
finally achieved in her poetry a complex and recursive sense of multiple identities. With these lines, Rich understands that the conflicts of her identity—
her "white, Jewish, anti-Semite, racist, anti-racist, once-married, lesbian,
middle-class, feminist, exmatriate southerner" (BBP 122) identities—are assets,
for they "breathe in me / as angels, not polarities" (WP 9). As "Integrity" comes
to a close, Rich comments that the boat she is moving on travels through "mis-
blotted sunlight, critical light / imperceptibly scalding / the skin these hands
will also salve" (WP 9). In the poem Rich has found that she can heal her own
pain even when inflicted by outside forces, and that in doing so she has found
"the quality or state of being complete" with which the poem begins.

Other poems in *A Wild Patience* examine Rich's "selves" in an attempt to
understand how she reached this point. Bennett correctly points out that many
of Rich's poems in this volume, and in *Sources,* which was first published as
a chapbook before being republished in *Your Native Land, Your Life* in 1986,
are written in an "interrogatory mode, questioning over and over again what
happened in the past and her relation to it" (236). Moreover, "it is the pieces of
herself, not just the lives of other women, that she is now attempting to bring
together" (Bennett 236). Numerous questions resound throughout the collection as Rich examines her personal location and influences. In "For Memory,"
for example, Rich travels back to her childhood, wondering what she has re-
membered and told people and what she has not. She understands that her past
is a place to which she must return and say *"this is where I came from / this
is what I knew"* (WP 22). "For Julia in Nebraska," discussing the respect and
dignity left by Willa Cather as a legacy for women, asks, "How are we going
to do better?" (WP 18). The poem "Transit" examines Rich's own battle with
rheumatoid arthritis as she compares her crippled body to an able-bodied skier.

Last, Rich finally asks the key question underlining much of the collection
in the poem "The Spirit of Place." Toward the end of the first section, Rich

plainly asks, "*With whom do you believe your lot is cast?*" (WP 41). The question, which will resound throughout the sequence poem "Sources" in *Your Native Land, Your Life*, centers Rich on her quest to discover who she is and how each fragment of her experience creates her identity. Is she supposed to cast her lot with her Jewish self, with the lesbian self, or with the white, middle-class self? The question could be neither avoided nor answered at this point in Rich's life and career. "The Spirit of the Place" also illustrates Rich's growing concern with the influence of history on identity. Here she moves away from the influences of the male-dominated literary past and turns to examine how the history of North America has been maintained in a patriarchal culture. The poem stands as a clear indication of Rich's later concerns to be found in *Your Native Land, Your Life* (1986); *An Atlas of the Difficult World* (1991); and *Dark Fields of the Republic* (1995), where Rich delves deeply into issues regarding national identity, cultural identity, cultural transgressions against people and the land, and the political power of poetry to effect change and responsibility.

Set in New England, "The Spirit of the Place" examines the way in which scholars have appropriated history for their own purposes, an action that Rich believed limits history's complexity as an influence on our lives. For example, as Templeton discusses, the third section of the poem returns again to the life of Emily Dickinson, and Rich criticizes the scholars who have taken over Dickinson's life with "their pious or clinical legends" that "festoon the walls like imitations / of period patterns" (WP 42). Rich desires to protect Dickinson from this invasion in her "third and last address to you" (WP 43). With the hands of a daughter, sister, and mother, Rich seeks to "cover [Dickinson] / from all intrusion" (WP 43). In the end the focus of the section in the poem is on "the scholars' pretense of knowing Dickinson, and Rich's rather exhausted desire to 'close the door' and protect Dickinson from all interpretive inquiries, even well-meaning ones, even Rich's own" (Templeton, *Dream and the Dialogue*, 104). The scholars' appropriation of Dickinson victimizes her, reducing her to an object only to be studied.

As a result Dickinson's life and work have become minimized for Rich, and she wishes to close all the doors, offering Dickinson the very seclusion and privacy she sought when she was living. Furthermore this victimization of Dickinson exists as a sign of the power that history holds to omit or appropriate women for its own purposes. We can begin to understand how history has influenced Rich here as the actions of the scholars prevent Rich from accessing a source of inspiration and personal power. Unwilling to be a part of the ongoing victimization, Rich stifles the desire to know and use Dickinson's life and work. Scholars' (mis)handling of historical figures, particularly women, has affected Rich in such a way that she can no longer look at Dickinson as she did in a poem such as "I am in Danger—Sir!," found in *Necessities of Life*.

In section 5 of "The Spirit of Place," Rich continues to examine the role of history in the formation of her identity in North America. Looking up at Orion and the other constellations, Rich remarks,

> All the figures up there look violent to me
> as a pogrom on Christmas Eve in some old country
> I want our own earth   not the satellites, our
>
> world as it is   if not as it might be
> then as it is: male dominion, gangrape, lynching, pogrom
> the Mohawk wraiths in their tracts of leafless birch
>
> watching: will we do better?
> The tests I need to pass are prescribed by the spirits
> of place   who understand travel but not amnesia (WP 44–45)

Rich's desire for a better world to come is palpable here. The poem questions the differences between facts and desires, while also criticizing the existing structures that enable male domination, violence against women, and oppression against minorities.

Yet, Rich also remained aware of her own failures to recover history and to accept responsibility for oppressions in the world, as seen in the section discussing Emily Dickinson and when she asks, "will we do better?" Furthermore, according to Bennett, the attempted appropriation of historical figures such as Dickinson "exposes determinism as delusory and allows [Rich] to loosen ideology while it brings her into community with other women" (106). The belief that decisions made by people simply happen and are unaffected by human will results in a knowledge of history that refuses to envision change and a different way of being. Bennett also argues that "historical discontinuity and indeterminacy are fundamental, indispensable, and joyful concepts in a feminist vision because they affirm the basic feminist assumption that choice and change are possible" (90). For that reason *A Wild Patience Has Taken Me This Far* can be seen as continuing Rich's lesbian-identified vision begun in *The Dream of a Common Language*. Rich's ability to understand the limitations of determinism allowed her to see change and independent choices as both possible and desirable.

Moreover, Rich recognized that she needed to examine her position in history in order to embrace her own fluctuating identities and the disparate influences on those identities. She concludes "The Spirit of Place" calling for understanding about the world we have created, not to "exact reparation for things / done long ago to us and to those who did not // survive what was done to them," but to honor them "with grief   with fury   with action" (WP 45). The people and the events of the past inevitably influence who we are today, and Rich calls for a new way of knowing and using the past. The repetition in the line "knowing   knowing   knowing" points to Rich's continuing desire for movement, for knowing the world and her place in it (WP 45).

CHAPTER 4

Entering History

A new phase of Rich's career emerged with the publication of *Your Native Land, Your Life* in 1986 as Rich turned to a close examination of her life and location within her country. This shift grew as Rich's poems in the late 1980s into the 1990s began to look outward at American history, as seen in *An Atlas of the Difficult World* (1991), *Dark Fields of the Republic* (1995), and *Midnight Salvage* (1999). Within these collections Rich considers what responsibility we have—individually and communally—for changing the conditions under which we live. In particular, the later works attend to Rich's charge that poetry, the unique language of a poem that can "uncover desires and appetites buried under the accumulating emergencies of our lives, the fabricated wants and needs we have had urged on us, have accepted as our own," carries the ability to create social change and to engage us in our democracy (WFT 13). As she moved through the time period of the 1980s to the end of the century, Rich's work also broadened beyond feminist poetics as she developed a national voice and a new role as a citizen poet.

Your Native Land, Your Life is a transformative collection in Rich's long career. The poems emerge from Rich's exploration of her personal experiences as well as her position within her country. Rich explains on the book's cover note, "In these poems I have been trying to speak from, and of, and to, my country. To speak a different claim from those staked by the patriots of the sword; to speak of the land itself, the cities, and of the imaginations that have dwelt here, at risk, unfree, assaulted, erased. I believe more than ever that the search for justice and compassion is the great wellspring for poetry in our time, throughout the world, though the theme of despair has been canonized in this century. I draw strength from the traditions of all those who, with every reason to despair, have refused to do so" (YNL back cover). As Rich engages her country through the lens of her personal experiences, she expands upon familiar topics, including the role and power of poetry to effect change, the tensions between the individual and community, and the search for an understanding of self-identity. These topics develop in the collection's three distinct sections. With the first section, a sequence poem titled "Sources," Rich examines her life to determine where she locates her individual strength. The second section, "North American Time," thrusts Rich into the public world as she debates the role of the poet and poetry and contemplates despair, justice, and communal responsibility. In the third section, "Contradictions: Tracking Poems," Rich returns to her personal experiences to draw connections from the body's pain and the world's pain in an effort to guide readers into examining their lives, their native land. *Your Native Land, Your Life* marked a significant shift in Rich's poetics as she turned toward a broader vision of her country.

Composed of twenty-three poems, the opening sequence "Sources" is an autobiographical work that asks a central question found in poem III:

> *From where does your strength come, you Southern Jew?*
> *split at the root, raised in a castle of air?*

Yes.   I expected this.   I have known for years
the question was coming.   *From where* (YNL 5)

In "Notes toward a Politics of Location," an essay Rich wrote three years after "Sources," Rich explains her focus on identity and location in North America: "As a woman I have a country, as a woman I cannot divest myself of that country merely by condemning its government or by saying three times 'As a woman my country is the whole world.' Tribal loyalties aside and even if nation-states are now just pretexts used by multinational conglomerates to serve their interests, I need to understand how a place on a map is also a place in history within which as a woman, a Jew, a lesbian, a feminist I am created and trying to create" (BBP 212). *Your Native Land, Your Life* resounds with questions and the desire to understand how one's identity is shaped by one's cultural contexts. Where does strength come from amid a diverse, patriarchal culture? When one is a woman? A Jew? A lesbian? White? How does a "place on a map," which is located in a particular historical context, influence who we are and what we think? And how does one's country impact one's identity and accountability in the world?

"Sources," the collection's first section, opens with a poem that returns Rich to Vermont and sets the tone for the sequence. While the poem suggests that it has been sixteen years since her last visit, Albert Gelpi, in "Poetics of Recovery: A Reading of Adrienne Rich's *Sources*," explains that the lapse of years moves backward from when the sequence was written in 1981–82 to 1965–66, a year that "stands now as a decisive turning point in her life" as Rich moved with her husband and children to New York City (397). As Gelpi notes, after 1965 Rich experienced significant events, including her participation in civil rights and antiwar protests, her work teaching at City University of New York's open-admissions program, her separation from her husband, his suicide, and her sons growing up (A. Gelpi, "Poetics of Recovery" 397–98).

Refusing "to become a seeker for cures," Rich states in poem II that her sources of strength already lie within her: "Old things, diffuse, unnamed, lie strong / across my heart" (YNL 4). Poem III questions that strength through italicized lines that repeatedly ask, *"From where?"* (YNL 5). Poem IV reveals Rich's search for personal understanding as well as her awareness that her poetry often touches on issues of identity and place. She rephrases the questions asked in poem 3: *"With whom do you believe your lot is cast? / From where does your strength come?"* (YNL 6). Rich clarifies these questions for us:

> I think somehow, somewhere
> every poem of mine must repeat those questions
>
> which are not the same.   There is a *whom,* a *where*
> that is not chosen   that is given   and sometimes falsely given
>
> in the beginning we grasp whatever we can
> to survive (YNL 6)

The "whom" and the "where" that are not chosen but given are the markers of identity with which one is born. As Rich has discussed, from the moment she was born, she recognized that she was marked by her race and gender. Further, as the poem notes, sometimes these markers are "falsely given" as they are imposed by cultural forces. In "Twenty-One Love Poems" from *The Dream of a Common Language,* Rich addresses such a false given in her celebration of the lesbian body, which directly opposes cultural norms dictating what Rich names "compulsory heterosexuality." In other earlier poems, such as "Snapshots of a Daughter-in-Law" and "Unsaid Word," Rich questions women's socially prescribed roles. Amid socially created forces, within the "Sources" sequence, Rich "grasps" what she can to ensure her survival.

Gender emerges in the "Sources" sequence as a primary source of strength that Rich grasps for survival. Within the sequence Rich confronts gender in a new way as she reflects upon her conflicted relationship with her father and how he represented patriarchy for her, as well as her relationship with her late husband. She writes in poem VII of her years struggling with her father, seeing herself as "the eldest daughter raised as a son" who "must overthrow the father, take / what he taught her and use it against him" (YNL 9). As an adult, Rich confronts her father again after he has died:

> After your death I met you again as the face of patriarchy, could
> name at last precisely the principle you embodied, there was an
> ideology at last which let me dispose of you, identify the suffering
> you caused, hate you righteously as part of a system, the kingdom
> of the fathers. (YNL 9)

Rich's lines reject her father as a symbol of a patriarchal culture that oppressed her. For Rich, her father was someone to blame for the situation in which she was born—a woman expected to fulfill certain roles throughout her lifetime. Yet as the poem continues, Rich documents how her anger has faded:

> I saw the power and arrogance of the male as your
> true watermark; I did not see beneath it the suffering of the Jew,
> the alien stamp you bore, because you had deliberately arranged that
> it should be invisible to me.   It is only now, under a powerful,
> womanly lens, that I can decipher your suffering and deny no part
> of my own. (YNL 9)

Seeing only the male watermark, Rich failed to acknowledge her father's humanity and his own conflicting identities. Only now, years after his death, can she understand his suffering and the struggle he had to fit into a culture that denied Jews—an oppression similar to her experiences as a woman. Rich explained this shift in perspective in an interview: "I've been thinking about my father more and more in the context of the social and political world that he grew up in, about the things that brought him to where he was when I knew him, especially the meaning of his Jewishness. He had been, for me, such an ambiguous figure, so tremendously rewarding, on the one hand, and also such an obstacle. Now, it's much more this person who had his own history and his own family background and parents who had a certain life themselves and who came from certain kinds of families, that they were Jews in the South in a particular period" (Montenegro 12). As Joanne Feit Diehl explains in *Women Poets and the American Sublime,* Rich's shift was influenced by a recognition of the need "to include the reimagining of a past that recognizes rather than rejects the sources of personal as well as cultural history" (155). With the inclusion of her father into the poem, as well as her newfound understanding of how his cultural context influenced his actions, "Rich incorporates the most threatening aspects of her past without subordinating her feminist sense of difference" (Diehl, *Women Poets* 155). Significantly, her new understanding of her father's position is filtered through a "womanly lens," suggesting that the gendered body offers a powerful way to understand social and political contexts and to possess empathy.

In poem XVII, Rich turns to her late husband as she considers the linkages between her father and husband, both Jews who sought to assimilate into the dominant culture while denying their religion. Rich reflects on her husband, who, like her father, "ended isolate, who had tried to / move in the floating world of the assimilated" (YNL 19). Rich reflects on how she put her father and husband in opposition to one another, as well as how she chose to marry a man unlike her father. As she notes, "I needed your unlikeness then" (YNL 19). But now, years later, Rich finds that her father's likeness "stares me in the face" as she recognizes that she carries his imprint with her (YNL 19).

Poem XXII continues Rich's memories of her husband, who committed suicide in 1976, an event she had never addressed previously in her writings. Noting that she has "resisted this for years, writing to you as if you could hear / me," Rich also explains, "I've had the sense of / protecting your existence, not using it merely as a theme for poetry / or tragic musings" (YNL 25). The poem's second section seeks to understand her husband, recognizing that he had a "formula" to "stand between [him] and pain" (YNL 25). Within the poem's third section, Rich speaks directly to her husband:

> That's why I want to speak to you now.   To say: no person,
> trying to take responsibility for her or his identity, should have to
> be so alone.   There must be those among whom we can sit down
> and weep, and still be counted as warriors.   (I make up this strange,
> angry packet for you, threaded with love.)   I think you thought
> there was no such place for you, and perhaps there was none then,
> and perhaps there is none now; but we will have to make it, we who
> want an end to suffering, who want to change the laws of history, if
> we are not to *give ourselves away.* (YNL 25)

Here, Rich suggests that individuals cannot survive without support. Drawing upon a theme from *The Dream of a Common Language,* Rich again calls for community, a place where people can reveal weakness yet not be cast out for doing so.

Significantly, Rich's choice to write about her husband as well as her father reveals another new source of strength as it demonstrates her newfound empathy for those outside of her. Albert Gelpi's "Adrienne Rich: The Poetics of Change" captures this important shift in Rich's work, commenting that as Rich reflects upon her past relationships with her father and her husband, she "finds that they no longer have any power over her, indeed finds that she can be compassionate and loving because she can now see them too as the victims of patriarchy, the individual but related weaknesses that defeated them now enmeshed in the circumstances of their lives" (299). Holding on to the memory of her husband, understanding the pain he suffered, pushes Rich to claim space for those who feel dispossessed, to continue her search for a community where people take responsibility for one another. In doing so, this poem for her husband creates "a stronger and more deeply empowered poetics based not on defense, but upon what Emerson, in an evocative phrase, described as the 'flames and generosities of the heart'" (Diehl, *Women Poets*, 159).

As noted in poem VII, where Rich raises the concept of a "womanly lens," Rich's sequence asserts that empathy, informed by her experiences as a woman, provides a powerful lens through which to view the world. The final poem of the sequence, which is unnumbered, captures Rich's mission moving forward:

> When
> I speak of an end to suffering I don't mean anesthesia. I mean know-
> ing the world, and my place in it, not in order to stare with bitter-
> ness or detachment, but as a powerful and womanly series of
> choices: and here I write the words, in their fullness:
> powerful;   womanly. (YNL 27)

Ultimately the "Sources" sequence situates Rich in a new position, one informed by her gendered body and her feminist vision for community. She concludes by announcing that she still believes in a "womanly series of choices," but it is not the radical lesbian-separatist vision that was developed in *The Dream of a Common Language* ten years earlier. Writing of the men in her life, opening a dialogue with them, Rich reveals a new belief that she cannot dismiss a section of humanity simply because it once dismissed her. Rich chooses to engage with patriarchal constructions, instead of against them, in order to understand fully the influences that have shaped her.

The primary factor driving Rich's vision was her recognition of her gendered body as a source of strength. In "If Not with Others, How?," an essay written in 1985, Rich writes about her thoughts on what it means to be outside of the cultural majority, reflecting on what it means to identify as a woman, a Jew, as a person of color. Rich puts forth her hope that the women's movement of the 1980s "can further the conscious work of turning Otherness into a keen lens of empathy, that we can bring into being a politics . . . of what it means to be Other" (BBP 203). She then provides a list of wide-ranging identities from women and men to those who are middle or working class to those who are "gay and straight and bisexual, older and younger, differently able and temporarily able-bodied" (BBP 203). Rich asserts her belief that despite individual differences, "we share an unquenched hope for the survival and sanity of the human community. Believing that no single people can survive being only for itself, we want a base from which to act on our hope" (BBP 203). "Sources" puts forward a call for empathy, for a coming together across individual differences, to shape the world.

Section 2, titled "North American Time," shifts from a personal reflection on self-identity and experience to the broader landscape of North America spurred by Rich's travels. Within this section Rich begins "to speak from, and of, and to [her] country" (YNL back cover). In the early 1980s Rich traveled to Nicaragua, a trip documented by a number of essays found in *Blood, Bread, and Poetry*. Throughout the trip Rich found herself meeting daily with women and men responsible for policy decisions. In the 1983 essay "North American Tunnel Vision," she explains that these people "sound as if they believe what they are saying" and are people who "speak with love and commitment to the needs of the poorest people" as they also speak about their country "in a language of concrete, unaggrandized simplicity—of its sufferings, its hopes, its beauty, its poverty, its smallness, its need to work out its own way in the world" (BBP 163). These interactions with the leaders of Nicaragua led Rich to realize that North Americans are "used to living in a naïve cynicism" (BBP 164). Further, Rich asserts that North Americans "shrug at the manipulations which are the daily life of this society; we do not expect sincerity in public life" (BBP 164).

This experience, among others, acted as a catalyst in Rich's work during the early 1980s. Many of her essays, among them "North American Tunnel Vision," "Resisting Amnesia: History and Personal Life," and "Notes toward a Politics of Location," indicate her growing awareness of and desire to speak about the actual actions and history of her country. As she asserts in "Resisting Amnesia: History and Personal Life," "As a woman, as a feminist, as a Jew, as a lesbian, I am pursued by questions of historical process, of historical responsibility, questions of historical consciousness and ignorance and what these have to do with power" (BBP 137). At this particular moment in time, Rich found herself considering change and possibility, an openness that appears to have originated in large part from her experiences in Central America. There she found herself thinking about new approaches to women's histories and identities as well as other concerns for women's lives. As she writes in "North American Tunnel Vision," she found herself having to think about women's issues "not just as reproductive issues or the problems of rape, woman battering, child abuse, but as literacy, infant mortality, the fundamental issue of having something to eat" (BBP 163).

These new concerns, which built upon existing concerns in the United States, enabled Rich to turn her own eye to history and how representations of history affect power relations in North America. For Rich, this decision was a deliberate one. In "Resisting Amnesia," she explains that "you do have a choice to become *consciously* historical—that is, a person who tries for memory and connectedness against amnesia and nostalgia, who tries to describe her or his journeys as accurately as possible. . . . Breaking silences, telling our tales, is not enough. We can value that process—and the courage it may require—without believing that it is an end in itself. Historical responsibility has, after all, to do with action—where we place the weight of our existences on the line, cast our lot with others, move from an individual consciousness to a collective one" (BBP 145).

The title poem of the collection's second section, "North American Time," stands out as a driving force for the collection as it captures Rich's expanding poetics that stem from her growing awareness of North America as a political power and her own location within her country. Rich occupies a position within the poem from the very start as she questions in the first stanza if her poems are becoming predictable with "no unruly images / escaping beyond borders" (YNL 33). The second stanza focuses on the responsibilities associated with writing as the poet recognizes that "Poetry never stood a chance / of standing outside history" (YNL 33); further, the poet understands that

> We move   but our words stand
> become responsible
> for more than we intended
>
> and this is verbal privilege (YNL 33)

Rich's lines assert that we are all responsible for the words we use or our silences. The stanza suggests that we each have a political responsibility to engage the world around us. In "Resisting Amnesia," Rich explains this responsibility: "we cannot help making history because we are made of it, and history is made of people like us, carriers of the behavior and assumptions of a given time and place" (BBP 144).

In the third stanza, Rich calls upon her readers to be more aware of what happens and how we remember what happens in the world. To do this, she moves from using "we" to using the more forceful and personal pronoun "you." Through direct address, Rich questions her readers as she asks them to examine how their individual contexts and locations influence how they see history:

> Try sitting at a typewriter
> one calm summer evening
> at a table by a window

in the country, try pretending
your time does not exist
that you are simply you (YNL 34)

Rich's recognition of our inseparability from history forces readers to (re)eval-
uate history. When Rich writes to her readers, "try telling yourself / you are not
accountable / to the life of your tribe / the breath of your planet," she suggests
that each of us is accountable for history (YNL 34). Since there is no avoiding
our own continual implication in how we see and (re)construct the world, we
must fully locate ourselves within it and consciously seek to understand how
we all exist as forces of influence.

However, Rich refuses to seek simply a feminist re-vision of history. Instead
she pursues a larger-scale understanding of how our histories affect us as she
speaks of the need to know what goes on in one's country. Only by knowing
"what country it happens in / what else happens in that country" do we have
the power to understand our experiences (YNL 35). The need for a historical
and cultural context is crucial to situating ourselves in history. "You have to
know these things," Rich states (YNL 35). In "Notes toward a Politics of Location," Rich explains herself more fully: "It was in reading poems by contemporary Cuban women that I began to experience the meaning of North America
as a location which had also shaped my ways of seeing and my ideas of who
and what was important, a location for which I was also responsible" (BBP
219–20).

Understanding the historical context was essential for Rich. In the sixth
stanza of "North American Time," she notes that "words— / whether we like
it or not— / stand in a time of their own" (YNL 35). She follows these lines
by suggesting that we cannot avoid responsibility for our words or justify that
they were written before something was known or events occurred. Rich lists a
myriad of historical names and events from the twentieth century. The historical names, such as Rosa Luxemburg, Malcolm X, Kollontai, and Anna Mae
Aquash, represent people who were murdered for their political actions. These
names are juxtaposed against a list of historical sites of social protest and
violence against human life, including Treblinka, Beirut, Soweto, Sharpeville,
Hiroshima, and Biafra, among others. This listing highlights Rich's focus on
historical context, "—those faces, names of places / sheared from the almanac
/ of North American time" (YNL 35). Our historical representations stand as
a testament to who we have been—an almanac recording the truths and losses
of a collective experience. Here, Rich's poem records the histories that continue
to define us in North America.

In doing so, Rich focuses her readers' attention on language, explaining that we cannot change what we wrote before these events occurred or after. "Words stand" and can be used against us even "where the context is never given / though we try to explain, over and over" (YNL 35). The importance of language, the power of language to translate moments in time, reveals itself through Rich's return, again and again, to the phrases "our words stand," "verbal privilege," and "words are found responsible." Centering on the power of language, Rich debates representations and perceptions by individuals and communities. Through language, Rich argues, we are exposed to our own histories as well as the histories of others. Therefore, Rich tells us, we are responsible for what we represent. As "our words stand," we must take responsibility for the images, beliefs, and values created through language since "there is no escaping our position, where we stand literally and metaphorically," and we cannot hope "to escap[e] history through language" (Meese, *ExTensions* 176).

The inability to escape comes out strongly in the final sections of "North American Time." There, in section VII, Rich reveals how she is overwhelmed by the work to be done, explaining that at times she feels that "what [she] must engage" is "meant to break [her] heart and reduce [her] to silence" (YNL 36). Confronting history, writing history, the poet must fight to survive as she accepts responsibility for what she has written and what she will write in the future. As she contemplates this fight for survival, Rich concludes the poem by speaking of the world we live in, illustrating how we need to look carefully and reflect upon how our world affects us:

> The almost-full moon rises
> timelessly speaking of change
> out of the Bronx, the Harlem River
> the drowned towns of the Quabbin
> the pilfered burial mounds
> the toxic swamps, the testing-grounds
>
> and I start to speak again (YNL 36)

The closing lines document sites in American history, the "pilfered burial mounds" of the Native Americans, the "toxic swamps" where we carelessly dumped material we chose not to safeguard people against, the political decision to flood four towns in Massachusetts to form the Quabbin reservoir, and the testing grounds where people are living and dying. These sites, the poem suggests, influence our identities and sense of place in America also. Rich's categorizing of these transgressions, coupled with her will "to speak again," refuses to allow us to accept where we stand.

Here, at the end of "North American Time," Rich indicates our need to revise our use of and sense of responsibility to the past if we are to create the future. While we cannot change the transgressions made against the land or the inability of people to accept responsibility for their actions, Rich suggests that we need to work with our mistakes. Just as Rich recognizes in *The Will to Change* that she needs to use the "oppressor's language" to talk to us, she suggests here that she must also question historical narratives manipulated by patriarchal powers and silence. As Rich asserts in *What Is Found There: Notebooks on Poetry and Politics,* "We must use what we have to invent what we desire" (215). With "North American Time, the poet who feared she may be reduced to silence returns once again to language to create what she desires. She "start[s] to speak again" knowing that her words are all she has to make sense of the world.

Making sense of the world requires hope, a sentiment expressed in "Dreams Before Waking," which opens with two epigraphs that guide the poem. The first epigraph is from Elie Wiesel: "Despair is the question" (YNL 44). The second epigraph, written in Spanish, comes from the Cuban poet and essayist Nancy Morejón: "*Hasta tu país cambió. Lo has cambiado tú mismo*" (YNL 44). Translated, the line reads, "Even your country has changed. You yourself have changed it" (YNL 113). The juxtaposition of the epigraphs establishes the poem's theme; if despair is to change, we must take action.

Once again Rich relies on direct address to the reader as the poem documents a life in a city filled with change. In this landscape, "Despair falls" (YNL 44) as new buildings block sunlight into homes, homeless people appear on the streets, hungry people search for food, and, even though you live "where still you can believe / it's the old neighborhood," you now "have your four locks on the door" (YNL 45). Situated with your "savings, your respectable past," the poem suggests that "you think you can make it straight through / if you don't speak of despair" (YNL 46). The poem challenges this stance in the closing stanza, asking questions of us: "What would it mean to live / in a city whose people were changing / each other's despair into hope?"; "what would it feel like to know / your country was changing?" (YNL 46). Each time the question is followed by a simple statement: "You yourself must change it" (YNL 46). The repetition of the statement reinforces Rich's message that each person is accountable to his or her time. As the poem closes, a final question is asked: "Though your life felt arduous / new and unmapped and strange / what would it mean to stand on the first / page of the end of despair?" (YNL 46). In typical Rich fashion, the poem does not offer remedies; rather, the poem places responsibility for creating change in the hands of people, a path that Rich would return to repeatedly in her future work.

This path is viable, Rich suggests, only through an understanding of not just our individuality but also our need for community, as seen in the poem "Yom Kippur 1984." According to George Hart, in "The Long Line in Rich's Recent Poetry," "Yom Kippur 1984" is an important poem as it marks Rich's "transition from a poet who, in her political and public poems, speaks to a specifically defined audience of women and political allies to one who addresses a national audience" (403). Hart argues further that it is with this poem in particular that Rich "begins to write, if not as a national poet, then at least as a poet addressing her nation" (403). The poem's central debate focuses on the poet's desire for solitude while also realizing a need to be part of the multitude. As Templeton points out, within the poem Rich questions the terms "multitude" and "solitude," as "*multitude* seems to denote a blurring of distinct forms, while *solitude* suggests a violent defense of some space called 'home'" (Templeton, *Dream and the Dialogue*, 128). Rich "rejects the false dichotomy"; in doing so, she shows that "to assert the value of solitude over the safety and political necessity of multitude can be misconstrued as dangerous and egotistical" (Templeton, *Dream and the Dialogue*, 128). In the end the poem raises the question of what it means to be an individual and yet to exist within a community.

We see this message take shape as Rich contemplates what it would mean to be alone and yet "not to feel lonely or afraid" (YNL 75). Further, the poem questions what it would be like to "wander far from your own or those you have called your own / to hear strangeness calling you from far away" (YNL 76). At the same time the poem calls for community:

> Find someone like yourself.   Find others.
> Agree you will never desert each other.
> Understand that any rift among you
> means power to those who want to do you in. (YNL 76)

Just as quickly the poem contradicts itself as the poet says, "I am trying to say / that to be with my people is my dearest wish" and yet continues, "I also love strangers / that I crave separateness" (YNL 77). Once again Rich offers no easy resolution here, and the desire for solitude is further complicated by the dangers that such separateness may bring, especially if one is not privileged. The poem documents those who are ostracized for not fitting into the dominant culture: the gay man "kicked into the icy / river"; the woman "dragged from her stalled car / into the mist-struck mountains, used and hacked to death"; the scholar "shot at the university gates on a summer evening" (YNL 77). Here those in solitude lack safety, leading the poet speaker to "want a gun to defend / you," as she searches for "what I can't have: / your elder sister, Justice" (YNL 77).

As the poem draws to a close, Rich poses two questions: "What is a Jew in solitude? / What is a woman in solitude, a queer woman or man?" (YNL 78). These questions are followed by several lines that outline different situations that bring together the outcast and the majority, mixing those in solitude with the multitude. When that happens, the poem asks, "what will solitude mean?" (YNL 78). Hart finds that this question thrusts Rich into a "prophetic and rhetorical mode," as she "speaks to a national audience as Whitman did, to celebrate and embrace, and as Jeffers did, to warn and condemn" (409). With "Yom Kippur 1984," Rich emerges with a broader vision for her poetry, building upon "North American Time" and the recognition that the poet, the user of words, is responsible for her country. She also sets up a new vision for her readers as the poem questions "what solitude might be in a new world, in which the disenfranchised return home and the blur of multitude sharpens into the distinct forms of individuals. In this new world justice would mean valuing the individual differences that belie any stereotyping by group" (Templeton, *Dream and the Dialogue*, 129). In this way the poem questions the relationship between the individual and community and how both might productively assert themselves in the world.

Your Native Land, Your Life concludes with a third section titled "Contradictions: Tracking Poems," a series of twenty-nine poems. Within this section Rich returns to personal experience, sharing with her reader the hardship of the road she has traveled for thirty-five years and the knowledge that she, who speaks so eloquently of the struggle for understanding one's identity, barely has hold of the subject material and the experiences of which she writes. In poem 15 Rich tells her readers "who think I find words for everything" that she is "barely / coming into possession of, invisible luggage / of more than fifty years" (YNL 97). While this luggage looks "at first / glance like everyone else's" at the "airport carousel," Rich knows that only she can pick up the pieces (YNL 97). Nobody will steal the luggage, the experiences that shape who she has been, who she is, and who she will become.

"Contradictions" also raises the specter of the aging, disabled body, particularly the pain that results from debilitating disease as Rich continues her desire to bring an end to suffering. She does this by connecting personal pain with the world's pain. Poem 7 in "Contradictions" takes on the subject of pain and is one of Rich's most personal poems, written as a letter to herself. There, Rich writes, "I feel signified by pain / from my breastbone through my left shoulder down / through my elbow into my wrist is a thread of pain" (YNL 89). The poem continues to document how Rich is typing the poem rather than writing it by hand due to the inflammation of her wrist that "blooms and rushes with pain / like a neon bulb" (YNL 89). Given this pain, the poet asks herself how she will live the rest of her life. Noting that "nothing is predictable with pain," Rich's refusal to give into the pain emerges at the end of the poem:

> But I'm already living the rest of my life
> not under conditions of my choosing
> wired   into pain
>   rider on the slow train (YNL 89)

Despite the pain, Rich continues forward, choosing to write; as Sylvia Henneberg comments in *The Creative Crone: Aging and the Poetry of May Sarton and Adrienne Rich,* Rich "does not let pain stop her from riding or, in this case, writing" (126). Further, while "unable to handwrite her poems, the poet turns to the typewriter, thereby 'changing weapons' rather than giving up the struggle" (Henneberg 126).

Subsequent poems in the "Contradictions" sequence touch upon the body's pain but do so in a less personalized form. For example, in poem 16 Rich connects herself to the American poet Elizabeth Bishop and her well-known poem "One Art," which discusses the "art of losing" (YNL 98). For Rich, loss is "no art / only badly-done exercises" as she questions the world. Rich notes that in the act of questioning, the self finds itself challenged by pain and loss:

> acts of the body forced to measure
> all instincts against pain
> acts of parting   trying to let go
> without giving up (YNL 98)

The body resists pain here in the struggle to let go of questions but not lose the energy to continue asking. Rich connects the body's pain with the process, concluding that there is "no art to this but anger" (YNL 98).

Poem 18 makes visible the connection that Rich is working to make between the individual body's pain and pain outside the body in "a world where pain is meant to be gagged / uncured   un-grieved-over" (YNL 100). Significantly, according to Henneberg, Rich does not link her pain to "inevitable and insurmountable aging and decline"; rather she "sees pain and incapacity as a challenge to transform the world around her, and by extension, herself. Loss of the well-functioning body and the pain accompanying such loss are certainly articulated, but such articulation carries the clear purpose of illustrating the political possibilities of pain" (125). Poem 18 continues, "The problem is / to connect, without hysteria, the pain / of any one's body with the pain of the body's world" (YNL 100). Rich's desire here is to recognize how an individual's pain may create a pathway to understand the pain of a world torn apart by violence and divisiveness, a theme she will develop further in *An Atlas of the Difficult World.*

Poem 19 turns back in on poem 18, as Rich states, "If to feel is to be unreliable / don't listen to us" and "if to be in pain is to be predictable / embittered bullying / then don't listen to us" (YNL 101). The poem challenges those who mistrust emotion, asserting also, "If we're in danger of mistaking / our personal trouble for the pain on the streets / don't listen to us" (101). As poem 19 moves to a close, the poet speaker strikes out at those who have freedom of movement, who unlike those who are "grounded" move too quickly to see the pain on the streets where "Trapped in one idea, you can't have feelings / Without feelings perhaps you can feel like a god" (YNL 101). In "Adrienne Rich's Identity Poetics: A Partly Common Language," Lynda K. Bundtzen comments that "throughout these poems, is a sense of Rich's body as a painful site from which to speak," with the poet existing in "an afflicted body" that she offers "as a metaphorical vehicle for the 'body's world'" (338–39). The "Contradictions" poems detail Rich's attempt to connect from her personal body and experiences to the world's body and histories. Drawing upon personal experience offers a pathway to engage the outer world.

The final poem of the "Contradictions" sequence outlines this pathway. Rich addresses her readers, "You for whom I write this," directly in the poem's second section: "in the night hours when the wrecked cartilage / sifts round the mystical jointure of the bones" and "when the insect of detritus crawls / from shoulder to elbow to wristbone" (YNL 111). Drawing again on personal experience of bodily pain, Rich urges her readers to

> remember: the body's pain and the pain on the streets
> are not the same   but you can learn
> from the edges that blur   O you who love clear edges
> more than anything   watch the edges that blur (YNL 111)

Through her personal pain Rich is able "to blur the edges between her identity and the many suffering others who inhabit these poems," suggesting that "the body in pain as a social and political entity is always carefully localized and historically situated" (Bundtzen 340). Here, Rich's poem suggests that it is not the clear edges that define us but the blurred ones. At the same time Rich urges her readers to "learn / from the edges that blur" for "there may be some overlap between an individual's pain and urban pain, homelessness, and the suffering of the poor. Blurred edges, like abridged principles, tell a story, show where to watch what's happening" (Langdell 177).

By integrating her personal experience into the "Contradictions" poems, Rich "transforms her physical suffering into a usable condition that allows her to connect with the suffering world" (Henneberg 126). This connection leads to what Rich identifies in *What Is Found There* as revolutionary art—art that has the power to move people to contemplate ideas they had not seen before. An essential element of revolutionary art, Rich tells us, is blurred edges. She writes, "This is its power: the tension between subject and means, between the *is* and what can be. Edges between ruin and celebration. Naming and mourning damage, keeping pain vocal so it cannot become normalized and acceptable. Yet, through that burning gauze in a poem which flickers over words and images, through the energy of desire, summoning a different reality" (WFT 242). In *Your Native Land, Your Life,* Rich has begun to summon that different reality; in doing so, she has also moved to draw her readers into the poetry to contemplate our own locations and responsibilities in our country.

Rich continues her examination of her native land and life in the 1991 collection, *An Atlas of the Difficult World.* The title of the collection points to Rich's expanding concerns with the world at large as she draws upon the metaphor of an atlas, which suggests not just the Greek myth of Atlas bearing the world upon his shoulders but also the idea of mapmaking and locating ourselves on a map in the world. Simultaneously, Rich also continues speaking to and from her country as the poems exemplify Rich's growing national voice. In an interview with Bill Moyers, Rich commented on the title poem from the collection and confirmed her growing national voice, noting that the poem "reflects on the condition of my country, which I wrote very consciously as a citizen poet, looking at the geography, the history, the people of my country" (345).

The first poem of the "Atlas" sequence alerts us that the woman we are encountering here is not the woman we have known in the past as Rich situates herself on the Pacific coast and writes, "—this is where I live now.   If you had known me / once, you'd still know me now though in a different / light and life.   This is no place you ever knew me" (ADW 4). Rich occupies new land in this collection and again moves forward to explore areas unfamiliar to her. While she has no desire to sift through the decay she sees in the country, she realizes that poetry provides the power to bring about change and a way to reimagine the constructs of society. Believing that "poetry can break open locked chambers of possibility, restore numbed zones to feeling, recharge desire," Rich demonstrates in her poems her ongoing desire to remap the world (WFT xiv). As Rich investigates her country's people, geography, and histories, she uses her poetry to guide her readers to a fuller understanding of their own politics.

As a result, *An Atlas of the Difficult World* emerges as another transformative moment in Rich's career. In her review of the collection, Mary Hussman asserts, "If Adrienne Rich stepped away from patriarchal society in her earlier books in order to establish her own voice as a woman, then with *An Atlas of the Difficult World* she steps fully back into contemporary society 'bent on fathoming what it means to love my country.' And that country includes men as well as women. Rich has discovered who she is; now she tries to show us where we are" (221). To help readers see "where we are," Rich guides readers through a myriad of issues confronting her country, among them war, poverty, social inequities, human degradation, individual loss and desire, and mortality.

The collection, as it leads readers through a map of our difficult world, has been described as "a road poem bearing witness" through which Rich "shows us places of beauty and squalor and people in all the complexities of human dignity and human degradation" (Hussman 222). Rich recognizes the difficulty of this journey:

> I don't want to know
> wreckage, dreck and waste, but these are the materials
> and so are the slow lift of the moon's belly
> over wreckage, dreck, and waste, wild treefrogs calling in
> another season, light and music still pouring over
> our fissured, cracked terrain. (ADW 4)

As she had done in previous collections, Rich understands that she must work with the materials she has at hand. Moreover, Rich is not afraid to question national identity and politics as she examines the "wreckage, dreck, and waste." This questioning is explained in the essay "Notes toward a Politics of Location," in which Rich comments, "'As a woman I have no country. As a woman I want no country. As a woman my country is the whole world.' These words, written by Virginia Woolf in her feminist and anti-fascist book *Three Guineas,* we dare not take out of context to justify a false transcendence, an irresponsibility toward the cultures and geopolitical regions in which we are rooted. . . . As women, I think it essential that we admit and explore our cultural identities, our national identities, even as we reject the patriotism, jingoism, nationalism offered to us as 'the American way of life'" (BBP 183). The opening sequence of *Atlas* offers insight into Rich's exploration of the nationalized body and American way of life. In a 1994 interview, Rich stated that with *Atlas*, "I was trying to talk about my location, the privileges, the complexity of loving my country and hating the ways our national interest is being defined for us" (Rothschild 34). We see this conversation emerge powerfully in the opening *Atlas* sequence as Rich is "bent on fathoming what it means to love my country" (ADW 22).

Poem II depicts a map of "our country" through a series of images that map the regions of the United States from the "desert where missiles are planted like corms," to the "breadbasket of foreclosed farms," to "the birthplace of the rockabilly boy," to the "cemetery of the poor / who died for democracy," as well as the sites where "fishing fleets / went bankrupt," the battlefields of Centralia and Detroit, and the "suburbs of acquiescence" (ADW 6). There are "other battlefields" depicted as well where citizens struggle to survive, particularly cities where jobs have been lost and manufacturing shut down (ADW 6). The lack of punctuation in the poem causes the images of despair to run rampant. Moreover the images of foreclosed farms, bankrupt fishers, and unemployed car workers indicate a land where financial stability and the American dream have been all but lost.

The poem offers a critique of capitalism, suggesting that it has negatively impacted the country as regional images are juxtaposed with "the suburbs of acquiescence   silence rising fumelike / from the streets" where there exists a "capital of money and dolor" (ADW 6). In "'Nothing Else Left to Read': Poetry and Audience in Adrienne Rich's *An Atlas of the Difficult World*," Piotr Gwiazda explains that this map presents the United States as "a country in crisis, haunted by financial instability, worker exploitation, and widespread poverty. It is not a land of prosperity and progress, but a tragic battleground scarred by age-old yet still unresolved political and social struggles" (174). Yet, Rich seemingly still holds out hope for this country she describes as she ends the poem dismissing small distinctions and calling upon people to recognize that North America is more than just a country or a map; rather the poem asserts that it is a mural and asks readers, "where do we see it from is the question" (ADW 6). This poem emerges as one of national damage, the move toward protectionism, the detailing of economic failures such as the conflict between the middle class and unionized loggers in Centralia in 1918. Rich's speaker situates herself in this history, calling upon readers to recognize how their personal locations influence not just how they see their country but also how they are part of the mural that creates the country.

Poem V of *Atlas* continues this exploration of nation, asking readers to "Catch if you can your country's moment, begin / where any calendar's ripped-off" (12). Rich's speaker goes on to catalog moments in American history that carry with them a legacy of violence: Appomattox, Wounded Knee, Los Alamos, Selma, Saigon. Each of these names calls forth memories of American actions ranging from the last battle of the Civil War in 1865; to Wounded Knee in 1890, where the American cavalry massacred the Lakota tribe; to the creation of the atomic bomb in Los Alamos in the 1940s; to the civil rights battles for voting and immigrant rights in Selma, Alabama. The list ends with Saigon, noting the last airlift of American civilians and military, along with Vietnamese civilians, in 1975.

In the midst of this history, Rich's speaker asks, "Where are we moored? What / are the bindings? What be- / hooves us?" (ADW 12). These questions push readers to situate themselves in history, to take on accountability for their nation's actions. In "Where We See It From: Adrienne Rich and a Reconstruction of American Space," William Waddell draws out the significance of these questions: "Where are we moored? It means in the poem something more like 'how do we orient ourselves toward these surroundings?' What perspective do we take, and how much kinship, community, or responsibility do we acknowledge? What is the source and ground of that consciousness? The question is finally less *spatial* than *ethical*. What behooves us? What must we do to ensure that the life we give our lives to will not be cheap, will not turn on us? How can we act on our desire for an end to suffering?" (95). The poem asks readers to question their responsibility for history, for their nation's identity in history. In "Resisting Amnesia: History and Personal Life," Rich asserts "that we cannot help making history because we are made of it, and history is made of people like us, carriers of the behavior and assumptions of a given time and place" (BBP 144). With *Atlas,* Rich puts the weight of the nation on her readers, asking them to determine what identities they will claim, what actions they will take.

In poem XI in *Atlas,* Rich further questions our locations in history, commenting on the disparate sense of community in a country fighting the first gulf war:

> Minerals, traces, rumors I am made from, morsel, miniscule
>   fibre, one woman
> like and unlike so many
> . . .
> One citizen like and unlike so many, touched and untouched in
>   passing
> —each of us now a driven grain, a nucleus, a city in crisis (ADW 22)

Rich grounds the individual in tactile imagery, moving from an individualized grain to an enclosed nucleus out to the larger confines of a city, as she then catalogs the multitude found in the city—ranging from those "constructing enclosures, bunkers, to escape the com- / mon fate," to "some who try to teach the moment, some who preach the / moment" (ADW 22), to "some for whom war is new, others for whom it merely continues / the old paroxysms of time," to "some for whom peace is a white man's word and a white man's / privilege" (ADW 23). This myriad of individuals reveals a nation composed of a multitude of differences. The identity of a country emerges from this sea of difference. Yet Rich does not stop there.

This imagery is followed by a firm reminder: "A patriot is not a weapon. A patriot is one who wrestles for the / soul of her country / as she wrestles for her own being" (ADW 23). Here Rich reclaims language, reminding us that the missiles of the gulf war are not the same as the patriot who fights for her country, who grounds her body in the vast differences of her country and the material experiences of her country. Gwiazda explains that with "this section Rich concentrates on the reluctance to question the government's policies if they are presented in the form of attractive war stories or war images" (177). Further, the poem presents Rich's interest "in the question of dissent: how to register one's opposition to the government and still be able to call oneself a patriot? With this gesture she alludes to the larger problematic of dissent in America, a question of growing importance in the twenty-first century as well, as America wrestles with its own self about its future identity" (Gwiazda 178).

Harkening back to the "Sources" sequence in *Your Native Land, Your Life*, Rich offers the following guiding lines for *Atlas:* "Where are we moored? / What are the bindings? What behooves us?" (ADW 12, 23). These lines force Rich's readers to confront their country and contemplate their own responsibility for their communities. The *Atlas* sequence concludes with poem 13 (Dedications), which reaches out to readers as Rich suggests that poetry might offer sustenance in this land of turmoil. Here Rich beckons to her readers as she pictures them reading the poem before leaving work, in a bookstore, or "in a room where too much has happened for you to bear" (ADW 25). She calls out to those finding "a new kind of love / your life has never allowed"; to those "who are counted out, / count themselves out, at too early an age"; to those who "read on" despite failing eyesight "because even the alphabet is precious" (ADW 25). For Rich, we turn to poetry because "life is short" and we "are thirsty" (ADW 26). She understands the solace readers search for in the poem:

> I know you are reading this poem listening for something, torn
>   between bitterness and hope
> turning back once again to the task you cannot refuse.
> I know you are reading this poem because there is nothing else
>   left to read
> there where you have landed, stripped as you are. (ADW 26)

Here Rich tells readers that we need poetry in order to reimagine the world. Stripped as we are, living in the "suburbs of acquiescence" (ADW 6), Rich pushes us to question the world we live in and says that poetry can help us see. In *What Is Found There: Notebooks on Poetry and Politics,* Rich explains why this act is important: "most often someone writing a poem believes in, depends on, a delicate, vibrating range of difference, that an 'I' can become a 'we' without extinguishing others, that a partly common language exists to which strangers can bring their own heartbeat, memories, images. A language that itself has learned from the heartbeat, memories, images of strangers" (85). This language, Rich's poems, calls upon her readers to look into the images and questions the mural of the country. At the end of *Your Native Land, Your Life*, in 1986, she compelled her readers to look into the "edges that blur" (YNL 111). With the *Atlas* sequence, Rich enables readers to do just that as she guides them to view the country as a mural that blurs differences and conflicts.

Viewing the country and people of a country as a mural provides the chance to discover new roads. In poem 5 Rich calls upon the poetry of Muriel Rukeyser and tells us,

> *There are roads to take* she wrote
> *when you think of your country*   driving south
> to West Virginia Gauley Bridge silicon mines the flakes of it
>   heaped like snow, death-angel white
> —poet journalist pioneer mother
> uncovering her country: *there are roads to take* (ADW 13)

The key is to find the best route amid the silicon mines, the foreclosed farms, the closed auto factories, and to decide how to live together in one country. Rich draws upon Rukeyser's words again in *What Is Found There*: "It isn't that one brings life together—it's that one will not allow it to be torn apart" (158). There are words and images that can help bring change—change that can be better brought about when we understand more fully what moors us, binds us, and behooves us in North America. As Rich concludes *An Atlas of the Difficult World*, she tells us,

> You are coming into us who cannot withstand you
> you are coming into us who never wanted to withstand you
> you are taking parts of us into places never planned
> you are going far away with pieces of our lives
>
> it will be short, it will take all your breath
> it will not be simple, it will become your will (ADW 57)

While the poem has been viewed as Rich's own confrontation with and understanding of her mortality as she reached her early sixties, the poem also suggests the power of poetry and the poet to effect change on a national level. Playing upon the "verbal privilege" she illustrates in *Your Native Land, Your*

Life, Rich's concluding poem expresses her belief that those of us who read and learn to understand our own politics of location will be able to engage in a similar recursive movement that she has followed throughout her lifetime. That ability to move back and forth between varying locations that influence our perspectives will allow people to understand the concept of a mural, to look into and value the blurring of edges in North America.

Published in 1995, *Dark Fields of the Republic* is Rich's thirteenth collection of poetry. As both Rafael Campo's "A Gift of Love and Light" and Mary K. DeShazer's "'The End of a Century': Feminist Millennial Vision in Adrienne Rich's *Dark Fields of the Republic*" point out, the collection establishes its focus through its epigraph taken from Fitzgerald's *The Great Gatsby:* "He had come a long way to this blue lawn, and his dream must have seemed so close that he could hardly fail to grasp it. He did not know that it was already behind him, somewhere back in that vast obscurity beyond the city, where the dark fields of the republic rolled on under the night" (DF n.p.). Like Fitzgerald, as she continues the work that began in *An Atlas of the Difficult World,* Rich sets out to critique North American society in a time of struggle and growing despair. In an effort to rescue lost dreams and to forge a new sense of communal responsibility, Rich exposes her readers to the cynicism and apathy that affect North America in the present. The life of the republic lies both behind and in front of us. Rich suggests that we simply need to identify the pieces that will help us move out of obscurity.

Rich's opening poem, "What Kind of Times Are These," signals to readers not just the themes of the collection but also the fact that her efforts to reach her readers cannot be as direct as she wishes. The title of the poem, which is also the title of the collection's first section, comes from a Bertolt Brecht poem. In the notes to *Dark Fields,* Rich provides Brecht's lines: "What kind of times are these / When it's almost a crime to talk about trees / Because it means keeping still about so many evil deeds?" (DF 75). DeShazer notes that while Brecht's "impassioned query resonates for Rich, she tilts his question slightly by insisting that as a U.S. poet writing at the end of the century, she *must* talk about trees if her audience is to listen at all" (38). "What Kind of Times Are These" opens with a seemingly innocent image of "two stands of trees where the grass grows / uphill" (DF 3). Yet near the trees lies an "old revolutionary road" in shadows "near a meeting-house abandoned by the persecuted / who disappeared into those shadows" (DF 3). The natural environment is disrupted by the memory of persecution, and Rich tells her readers in the next stanza, "this isn't a Russian poem, this is not somewhere else but here, / our country moving closer to its own truth and dread, / its own ways of making people disappear" (DF 3). DeShazer suggests that Rich defines her writing task here and goes against the grain since her "subjects are revolution, persecution, community; and that her poetry will be centered on particular places where she has walked 'at the edge of dread' rather than on vague abstractions" (38–39). Moreover, Rich carefully tells her readers that the poem is located here in North America and goes on to indict those who carelessly and purposefully make livings off of others, especially their country: "I won't tell you where the place is" as "I know already who wants to buy it, sell it, make it disappear" (DF 3).

Rich confronts those citizens consumed by material desires as she also clearly positions herself as a protector of the republic—a person not swayed by capitalism or politics. At the same time, as DeShazer asserts, Rich "refuses to participate in the appropriation of this country's human or natural resources by capitalism run amok; hence she imposes a rhetoric of withholding: for safety's sake, she will protect certain dangerous secrets" (39). While those secrets are not revealed in this opening poem, Rich's efforts to conceal are apparent. The place remains unidentified, an action reinforced by the final stanza of the poem: "And I won't tell you where it is, so why do I tell you / anything? Because you still listen, because in times like these / to have you listen at all, it's necessary / to talk about trees" (DF 3). In responding to Brecht's poem. Rich alters Brecht's lines to suggest that in this day and age, when a country is unable to stir itself from apathy and cynicism, a poet must talk about trees in order to get readers to listen. In doing so, Rich enacts her own hope expressed in *What Is Found There: Notebooks on Poetry and Politics* for poetry to remain unaffected by the material world: "Perhaps this is the hope: that poetry, by its nature, will never become leashed to profit, marketing, consumerism" (39). The poem stands in opposition to consumerism and profit while also noting Rich's understanding that she must carefully phrase her words and images if she is to be the public's voice.

"In Those Years," the second poem of *Dark Fields of the Republic,* contemplates the tensions between the individual and the community, between the personal and the public, returning to a theme from *Your Native Land, Your Life.* The poem opens with Rich noting, "In those years, people will say, we lost track / of the meaning of *we,* of *you* / we found ourselves / reduced to *I*" (DF 4). The poem acknowledges the choice to settle for personal experience, noting that this "was the only life / we could bear witness to" (DF 4). With the second stanza, however, this personal life is infringed upon by the public life as the "great dark birds of history screamed and plunged / into our personal weather" (DF 4). Even though the birds do not land, their presence seeps through fog to a shoreline "where we stood, saying *I*" (DF 4). While people desire to have personal lives, separate from the influences of the public, the poem questions the isolation of the individual in the face of history, suggesting that we individually cannot withstand the ongoing rush of history's influence.

Rich further considers the individual and our connection to a communal history in the six-poem sequence titled "Inscriptions," which concludes the collection. In "Poem Two: Movement," Rich suggests that history is a current that moves in and around us and that we must engage if we are to understand our public and private identities as citizens in North America. The first stanza of "Movement" establishes this vision:

> Old backswitching road bent toward the ocean's light
> Talking of angles of vision   movements   a black or a red tulip
>   opening
> Times of walking across a street   thinking
> not *I have joined a movement* but   *I am stepping in this deep current*
> *Part of my life washing behind me   terror I couldn't swim with*
> *part of my life waiting for me   a part I had no words for*
> *I need to live each day through   have them and know them all*
> *though I can see from here where I'll be standing in the end.* (DF 61)

"Poem Three: Origins" reinforces the fluidity needed to engage the world; as the poem asserts, a life does not unfold in one identifiable direction. Rather, "it moves / in loops   by switchbacks loosely strung / around the swelling of one hillside toward another / one island toward another" (DF 63). Through this switchback imagery, Waddell argues that Rich's poem shows how "our roads, turning back upon themselves, change our angles of vision, where we see things from. And in the image's spatial expression of time, moreover, Rich crafts an image of a perspective that can bring figures from our personal and national pasts into the same plane, blurring and even collapsing divisions of time" (97). Different angles of vision are required to move with the world.

The sequence poem "Calle Visión" pushes readers to contemplate these different angles of vision. Calle Visión is the name of a road in the southwestern region of the United States and translates as "vision street" (DF 76). A central image in the poem depicts a chicken slaughterhouse and the repetitiveness of the work that causes "fire in your wrist" and "carpal tunnel" (DF 16). Drawing upon an actual event, the poem closes with images of a fire that destroyed the factory, after which workers' bodies were found "fleeing to the freezer some / found 'stuck in poses of escape'" (DF 16). The poem forces readers to confront the material realities of the factory workers' lives.

We see another angle of vision in the section titled "Then and Now," a sequence of five poems that Rich explains developed from her reading of letters of Hannah Arendt, a political philosopher who escaped the Holocaust and became an American citizen, and Karl Jaspers, a German philosopher and psychiatrist (DF 78). The section opens with an epigraph: "Is it necessary for me to write obliquely / about the situation? Is that what / you would have me do?" (DF 25), which references the opening poem of the collection, where Rich asserts that she needs to talk about trees to get people to listen. Within the sequence Rich depicts Arendt's sending of food packages to Jaspers after World War II ended, along with the feelings of loss and guilt provoked by the war. In "Innocence: 1945," the poem's speaker comments, "We had done nothing while some / extreme measures were taken," and yet "we had suffered too" (DF 28). In "Sunset, December, 1993," Rich inserts personal experience as she links her act of writing to Arendt's and Jasper's, recognizing the dangers of writing in times of political upheaval and yet also questioning if it is more

> Dangerous not to think
>
> how the earth still was   in places
> while the chimneys shuddered with the first dischargements (DF 29)

The image here suggests the chimneys in the Nazi concentration camps and the need to remember past historical transgressions.

The sequence's closing poem, "And Now," captures the new space that Rich had carved for herself through *Your Native Land, Your Life, An Atlas of the Difficult World,* and *Dark Fields of the Republic,* three collections that together document Rich's shift to the role of citizen poet. She continually asserts in *Dark Fields of the Republic* that what she now writes for and about is us, her readers, in an effort to help us understand our private and public identities, our relationships to and accountability for history. She tells us in the poem "And Now,"

> I tried to listen to
> the public voice of our time
> tried to survey our public space
> as best I could
> —tried to remember and stay
> faithful to details, note
> precisely how the air moved
> and where the clock's hands stood
> and who was in charge of definitions
> and who stood by receiving them
> when the name of compassion

> was changed to the name of guilt
> when to feel with a human stranger
> was declared obsolete. (DF 31)

Here, Rich raises again the question from "In Those Years" about how we have lost a sense of community and empathy for the differences outside of our selves. Further, in *A Human Eye: Essays on Art in Society, 1997–2008*, Rich's opening preface draws upon Karl Marx's description of "how in the compulsive expansion of capital human senses become starved, reduced to the mere sense of ownership" (x). According to Rich, Marx "also observed: 'The eye has become a *human* eye only when its object has become a *human*, social object.' When art—as language, music, or in palpable, physically present silence—can induce that kind of seeing, holding, and responding, it can restore us to our senses" (*A Human Eye* x).

We can read Rich's "I" in the first line of the poem as a human "eye." In "Calle Visión," she tells us that she wears a "triple eye" as she walks the road and "past, present, future all are at [her] side" (DF 19). With *Dark Fields of the Republic,* Rich outlines her poetic mission as she positions the citizen poet as one who records history and the varying angles of vision that we must learn to see the world from if we are to confront the dark fields of our country. Since the publication of *Your Native Land, Your Life* in 1986, Rich had transformed into a citizen poet facing down the dark fields of the republic—a revolutionary poet who, in Rich's own words at the conclusion of *What Is Found There,* "loves people, rivers, other creatures, stones, trees inseparably from art, is not ashamed of any of those loves, and for them conjures a language that is public, intimate, inviting, terrifying, and beloved" (250).

CHAPTER 5

Poetry and Politics

In a 2011 interview with Kate Waldman, Rich offered a broad picture regarding the concerns of her writings: "I can see, in my eighties, that my work has been a search for the means—the instruments—to make art from insistent concerns and desires that I couldn't necessarily reach for in any other way. I wanted an awareness of the world as history, to put it largely—as made by human needs and minds and labors—and affections (and also by human cruelty and avariciousness)." This statement presents a different view of Rich, as she has often been seen as a feminist poet. As Rich's voice fully transformed from a feminist voice to a national voice, this focus on poetry as a way to interrogate the world developed further in collections published from 1999 to 2011: *Midnight Salvage* (1999); *The School Among the Ruins* (2004); *Telephone Ringing in the Labyrinth* (2009); and *Tonight No Poetry Will Serve* (2011). While Rich remained concerned with issues of gender, race, sexuality, oppression, and violence, among others, she also moved to broadly contemplating an American life in an increasingly global world. Her self-reflective statement as she neared the end of her life indicates a larger vision, one that is focused on how art, in particular poetry, can speak to our lives as we are part of and made by history, by individual and communal actions.

In *The Creative Crone: Aging and the Poetry of May Sarton and Adrienne Rich*, Sylvia Henneberg identifies Rich's later work as "an energetic phase of movement between charting the state of the world and seeking ways to extract political meanings from her findings, be they testimonies of joy or suffering" (121). This movement reveals itself in poems that seek to confront injustice, to make sense of how the individual and the community connect, to question how we can make sense of our surroundings. Further, Rich's later poems are less driven by answers than by questions. Relying on images, allusions to historical moments and people, and strategies that call upon readers to make meaning out of the texts, the poems model the questioning and dialogue that are necessary for democracy to flourish.

As Rich's later work unfolds, this larger vision is guided by her long-held belief that poetry possesses the power to create social change. For Rich, poetry "wrenches around our ideas about our lives as it grows alongside other kinds of human endeavor. But it also recalls us to ourselves—to memory, association, forgotten or forbidden languages" (WFT 234). Further, Rich believes that poetry as noted previously "can uncover desires and appetites buried under the accumulating emergencies of our lives, the fabricated wants and needs we have had urged on us, have accepted as our own. It's not a philosophical or psychological blueprint; it's an instrument for embodied experience" (WFT 13). Through the embodiment of experience, Rich argues that poetry draws readers in and helps them understand the world: "We go to poetry because we believe it has something to do with us. We also go to poetry to receive the experience of the *not me,* enter a field of vision we could not otherwise apprehend" (WFT 86).

Moreover, as Rich asserts, "Poetry is not a resting on the given, but a questing toward what might otherwise be" (WFT 234). In *Line Break: Poetry as Social Practice,* James Scully discusses the concept of dissident poetry, which offers a lens for viewing Rich's later work. According to Scully, dissident poetry "does not respect boundaries between private and public, self and other. In breaking boundaries it breaks silences: speaking for, or at best *with,* the silenced; opening poetry up, putting it in the middle of life rather than shunting it off into a corner. It is poetry that talks back, that would act as part of the world, not simply a mirror of it" (4). As can be seen in Rich's poems from the collection *Midnight Salvage* to her final collection, *Tonight No Poetry Will Serve,* she engages in writings that interact with the world and in so doing calls upon her readers to engage that world as well.

Midnight Salvage, published in 1999, follows in the Rich tradition with poems that address political inequities, violence, and the power of poetry, as seen in "Shattered Head," "Camino Real," and "Letters to a Young Poet," while also including poems that interweave her personal experiences such as those seen in "Seven Skins." There are also poems, such as "Char" and "Modotti," that depict the lives of historical figures. As she had in previous collections, Rich invites readers to reflect on their individual and collective accountability to the worlds in which they live as well as question what tools we need to sustain democracy. The collection's epigraph speaks to Rich's vision as she quotes a letter from the American poet George Oppen to his sister, June Oppen Degnan: "I don't know how to measure happiness. The issue is happiness, there is no other issue, or no other issue one has a right to think about for other people, to think about politically, but I don't know how to measure happiness" (MS n.p.). Rich explained the use of this epigraph in an interview from 1999. There she commented on Oppen's statement: "what he's talking about there is really what Hannah Arendt talks about in one of her essays—public happiness. A happiness of true participation in society, which would be possible for everyone" (Klein).

"Camino Real," a letter to readers, picks up on this concept of happiness:

> happiness is in itself a magical study
> a glimpse of the *unhandicapped life*
> as it might be for anyone, somewhere
>
> a kind of alchemy, a study of transformation
> else it withers, wilts (MS 32)

True participation in society is a necessity; without it, the poem suggests, society "withers, wilts" (MS 32). Part of this public happiness can be created, the collection argues, if we not only locate ourselves within history but also actively participate in shaping that history. In "A Long Conversation," Rich creates a multivoiced discussion that ebbs and flows through an examination of capitalism and the modern technological world, blending the voices of Marx, Guevara, Wittgenstein, and Coleridge, among others. The conversation in some ways represents Rich's own long conversation with poetry and language, the struggle "between persistence and impatience" (MS 54).

The poem is also about the voices poetry draws upon to create its images: the woman who asks, "Can we say if or how we find this true in our lives today?"; another voice who says, "Technology's changing the most ordinary forms of human contact—who can't see that, in their own life"; and another who responds, "But technology is nothing but a means" (MS 59). The poem's multiple voices expose the range of individual experiences that shape a democracy. While these layered voices depict the contradictory impulses in our communities, their intersections and disputes, they also demonstrate a common impulse central to democracy: that of dialogue and the exchange of individual viewpoints. In her portrayal of these impulses, Rich demonstrates how poetry provides an angle to understanding the individual within the community. Moreover the poem breaks down the walls between individuals, enabling them to imagine each other's experiences, which enables an understanding of difference, a long-sought-after Rich ideal.

With "Letters to a Young Poet," a series of seven poems, Rich addresses the power of poetry to confront daily realities. The speaker in the poem is the voice of poetry itself as it speaks to a young poet, a counterpart. The voice comments that they are both driven by the word "ineluctable" as they

> won't get quit
> of this: the worst of the new news
>
> history running back and forth
> panic in the labyrinth (MS 25)

The poem moves on to question what influence poetry possesses—does it "live its own life"? (MS 26). Or, as the voice of poetry asks the young poet,

> if a woman as vivid as any artist
> can fling any day herself from the 14th floor
>
> would it relieve you to decide   *Poetry*
> *doesn't make this happen?*" (MS 26)

The poem seemingly suggests that poetry is not connected to life decisions. However, simultaneously the poem asserts that poetry shapes consciousness. Rich confirmed this assertion in an interview with Matthew Rothschild: "I happen to think [poetry] makes a huge difference. Other people's poetry has made a huge difference in my life. It has changed the way I saw the world. It has changed the way I felt the world. It has changed the way I have understood another human being." Poetry, Rich argues, possesses the power to move us, as well as to help us understand the world, a sentiment apparent in the closing lines of the fourth poem in the sequence: "Look: with all my fear I'm here with you, trying what it / means, to stand fast; what it means to move" (MS 27).

At the same time the collection bears witness to violence and human suffering, as seen in the poem "Shattered Head." The poem rests on the image of a shattered head left lying on a wooded hill. Its silent resting offers a subtle critique of the world's violence through the poem's graphic imagery seen in the "(porridge of skull splinters, brain tissue / mouth and throat membrane, cranial fluid)" (MS 21). These lines confront readers with harsh violence, assaulting them with the brutality of the image. As Rafael Campo writes in "Exemplary Poet," Rich's "words and images ricochet off one another, as if the bullets and grenades of the killing fields were flying around us. When we are struck by her precision, we, too, feel wounded" (43). While readers may wish to immunize themselves from such violence, the poem's imagery pushes readers to see the condemnation of oppression. In doing so, the poem forces readers to react, which is one of Rich's central goals. For Rich, "In more ways than one, poetry must recall us to our senses—our bodily sensual life and our sense of other and different human presences. The oceanic multiplicities of this art call us toward possibilities of relation still very much alive in a world where violent material power can speak only to and of itself, yet in which, in the words of the Salvadorean revolutionary poet Roque Dalton—'poetry, like bread is for everyone'" (WFT 273).

The title sequence poem of *Midnight Salvage,* which opens with the image of a local salvage yard, offers a guiding metaphor for the collection. Salvage yards serve as repositories for used, damaged, or unwanted goods that are often recycled or reused by one who sifts through the objects to find something of use. The salvage yard metaphor, as a frame for the collection, suggests that the poems within contain ideas to encourage collective engagement. The sense of collective responsibility may help to overcome the despair and apathy characterizing contemporary democracy. Poem 3 suggests to readers how this collective responsibility might be created. There Rich admits that while she never expected hope to "form itself / completely in my time," she did hope that she "was conspiring, breathing-along / with history's systole-diastole," taking part in the heartbeat of the country (MS 10). The poem situates the individual as part of the systolic and diastolic movements of history, the ways in which our political acts, communities, and individual lives both contract and expand in time.

The sequence's fourth poem underscores the difficulties of this movement, particularly in a time when democracy is foundering as a "dreadnought wreck cut loose / from all vows, oaths, patents, compacts, promises" (MS 11). The wreck is democracy, cut loose from the hopes and promises that once propelled it forward. In closing, the seventh poem in the sequence carries a warning to readers that living within this wreck is not simple and requires "patience which waits for the language for meaning for the / least sign" of what we can salvage from history to move us forward. Rich firmly ends the sequence in the seventh poem writing, "*I will / submit to whatever poetry is / I accept no limits*" (MS 14). As she does so, Rich challenges her readers to accept no limits, to enter the stream of history, and to salvage what can be used for creating the future.

The 2004 collection, *The School among the Ruins,* develops Rich's look at our need for poetry and the need to confront the violence of the world with poems that draw upon 9/11, the Iraqi war, the Israeli-Palestinian conflict, and the United States as they confront war, terrorism, public apathy, the loss of communal responsibility, and the failure of language to create change. Leading up to the writing of the collection's title poem in the summer of 2001, Rich "had been reading accounts of 'civilian agonies' in Sarajevo, Baghdad, Bethlehem, Kabul"—readings that made her think, "We here could not expect to feel invulnerable forever" (Benson). With its epigraph, the title poem situates us in that history, as well as in a position of vulnerability: "*Beirut.Baghdad.Sarajevo.*

Bethlehem.Kabul. Not of course here" (SAR 22). The epigraph captures the sentiment that violence happens in other places, not in the United States. The poem opens with images of life in a town—children "flow / in columns at the doors" of the school, a place where there is "order without cruelty" (SAR 22). The poem's second section documents the town and school under attack from missiles, surrounded by "human debris" as "fear vacuums out the streets" (SAR 22). The teachers strive to maintain some semblance of normalcy for the children as they spend day and night in the school even as supplies dwindle and the children ask questions that the teachers cannot answer and want food that is no longer available.

While the children are told that they cannot go home but that they "aren't lost / this is our school," the poem shifts with the depiction of a cat, and a momentary connection takes place between the children and the animal (SAR 24). The cat is hungry also, but she can find mice to eat. The children name her, deciding that when they have milk, "we'll give her some" (SAR 24). This moment of intimate connection is followed by the poem's suggestions to readers how to survive in such violence: keep hope ("Maybe tomorrow the bakers can fix their ovens"); hold onto language ("We sang them to naps told stories"); hold onto emotion ("Don't let your faces turn to stone"); ask questions ("Don't stop asking me why") (SAR 25). In Rich fashion, the poem refuses to accept stasis, to not push back against our circumstances, to not question the times in which we live.

In discussing the experience of poetry, Rich explains, "The reading or hearing of a poem can transform consciousness, not according to some pre-ordered program but in the disorderly welter of subjectivity and imagination, the seeing and touching of another, of others, through language" (WFT xvi). Within "School among the Ruins," the poem challenges what is and what can be, while pushing for the need to hold on to our humanity, a connection created in and through language. At the same time, the poem refuses to accept the current circumstances as it concludes with the teachers guiding the children as they sing to them, tell stories, and play games. Most importantly, the teachers and children "sat learning by heart the names / some were too young to write / some had forgotten how" (SAR 25). As such, the poem ends on a call for language, the need to preserve language, as a tool for survival.

The long poem "USonian Journals 2000" stands as the centerpiece of *School Among the Ruins*. The poem not only furthers Rich's questioning of the times we live in, where people avoid responsibility, but also reiterates the need to hold on to language. The use of the word "USonian" is significant. The word carries two meanings depending on how it is used, either as an adjective suggesting someone or something is of or related to the United States or as a noun indicating one is an inhabitant of the United States. Thus the title "USonian Journals 2000" grounds the poem in the United States in the opening years of the twenty-first century. The historical context of "USonian Journals," which was written from 2000 to 2002, is significant as well. In the United States those years were a time of considerable upheaval, with an uncertain presidential election in 2000 that was decided by the Supreme Court, terrorist attacks on 9/11, and a year leading up to the start of the Iraq war in 2003. During this time, putting forth opinions that countered the government's actions was viewed as unpatriotic in a country that saw itself under attack. Rich's poem ultimately questions that sentiment, which she debunks in a 2002 article for *The Nation*: "To be 'antiwar' is to be for public debate and knowledge, the foundations of democratic polity" ("Making the Connections" 6).

Written like a journal, with shorthand and disparate passages, the poem opens with the journal writer experiencing a "Citizen/Alien/Night/Mare" as the country she inhabits "undergoes rapid and flagrant / change" and where she now feels like "a stranger" who is "no longer connected / along any continuous strand to the nature of the change" (SAR 37). This journal writer then moves to a new entry, "Day/Job/Mare." Here she has lunch with a friend and finds it difficult to connect. The friend gossips about coworkers, and when asked about the "cur- / rent Brit. labor scene; she talks about the influence of the indus- / trial revolution on Victorian prose" (SAR 37). The journal writer thinks that she needs to "get clear of this / find another day job" (SAR 37). The lack of connection between the two women is highlighted further when after lunch they are caught in an explosion of violence on the streets. While the friend runs toward the police, the journal writer chooses to run away. Within the opening sections, the poem reveals tensions that exist in a changing time in a post-9/11 world. The poem's speaker feels lost, while the two women cannot connect. Violence then impedes daily lives. Through this disjointed scene, the poem depicts the dissonance that can fragment individual relationships; further, the women's separate reactions to the violence suggest a loss of responsibility for one another, a social contract no longer followed.

The poem proposes that this lack of connection stems from a loss of language. The journal writer's comments are pointed directly to us, the readers:

I'd like you to see how differently
we're all moving, how the time allowed to let things become
known grows shorter and shorter, how quickly things and people get replaced. How interchangeable it all could get to seem.
Could get to seem . . . the kind of phrase we use now, avoiding the
verb *to be. There's a sense in which,* we say, dismissing other senses. (SAR 38)

The journal writer recognizes how fast-paced change has impacted our ability to connect. Further, the passage outlines how people avoid accountability as they hide behind empty phrases such as "could get to seem" and "there's a sense in which" rather than direct, active statements.

At the same time, the poem's journal writer reflects on why she ran away from authority rather than toward it when the violence occurred: "Having seen nothing I could swear to I felt at peace with my / default," she writes. "I would, at least, not be engaged in some mess not my / own" (SAR 38). The journal writer notes that she is complicit in the avoidance of public responsibility, telling us, "This is what I mean though: how differently we move, rap- / idly deciding what is and isn't ours. Indifferently" (SAR 38). The journal writer's actions, or lack thereof, suggest a breakdown in personal and public accountability. Further, the speaker's inability to connect, as well as her refusal to engage, suggests that public apathy has become the norm.

At the root of this apathy is the loss of language, a long-held Rich theme. The next section of the poem, titled "Voices," depicts the journal writer listening to a myriad of voices in a public mall and her overhearing of a neighbor's phone call conversation. Reflecting on the experiences, the journal writer contemplates "Private urgencies made public, not collective, speaker within a bubble" (SAR 39). This is "USonian speech," with which men need "to sound boyish" and women are "screeking to an excitable edge / of brightness" (SAR 39). Further, in "an excessively powerful country, grown women / sound like girls without authority or experience. Male, female / voices alike pitched fast-forward commercial, one timbre, tempo, / intonation" (SAR 39). Language fails in this section, as it conforms to one level, one speed, one tone. In *Arts of the Possible,* Rich discusses how language has been taken over by capitalism and "in the interests of marketing, distinctions fade and subtleties vanish" (149). Further, Rich argues that such a "devaluation of language, this flattening of images, results in a massive inarticulation, even among the educated. Language itself collapses into shallowness" (*Arts of the Possible* 149). The journal writer's experience speaks to that shallowness and the subsequent loss of real communication.

This lack of connection and communication continues in the poem as people in a gallery move about without "exchanging looks" while viewing images of the past, images no longer recognizable. Further on, the journal writer documents again the lack of communication:

No one is monitoring this conversa-
tion but us. We know the air is bad in here, maybe want not to
push that knowledge, ask *what is to be done?* How to breathe?

What will suffice? Draft new structures or simply be aware? If
art is our only resistance, what does that make us? If we're col-
laborators, what's our offering to corruption—an aesthetic,
anaesthetic, dye of silence, withdrawal, intellectual disgust? (SAR 41)

The poem suggests a complicity on the part of readers and the journal writer
alike, offering up a subtle critique that each of us who is not using language
to create change, to take action, is contributing to our "moribund democracy"
(SAR 41). The poem asks readers if it is enough or do we need to "draft new
structures" if we are to breathe fresh air?

As what "might reanimate, rearticulate" becomes "less and less available,"
the greater the public's apathy and isolation (SAR 41). The poem draws to an
end with a "Mission Statement," asserting Rich's conviction that *It is obvious
that the destruction of despair is still our most urgent task"* (SAR 42). Despair,
for Rich, is tied to loss of language, as she explains in *What Is Found There:*
"We hear despair in the loss of vitality in our spoken language: 'No problem,'
we say, 'that was a healing experience,' we say, 'thank you for sharing that,' we
say. We see despair in the political activist who doggedly goes on and on, turning in the ashes of the same burnt-out rhetoric, the same gestures, all imagination spent. Despair, when not the response to absolute physical and moral
defeat is, like war, the failure of imagination" (WFT 17). Rich's statement captures the ways in which language has lost meaning as people use phrases that
fail to create connections between people. To move beyond despair, "USonian
Journals 2000" proposes that we must reclaim language through those who are
"especially calibrated toward language" as they know its "known and unknown
powers / to bind and to dissociate"; its ability to "ostracize the speechless";
"to nourish self-deception"; to foster "rebirth and subversion"; and above all,
"because of the history / of torture / against human speech" (SAR 43).

For Rich, the poet is one calibrated to do this work as the poem ends with
a call to readers to remember the power of language—to recalibrate our use
of language, to question authority, our government's practices, and our own
actions. Through language, the poem argues, we can end despair, recapture
imagination, and return to a citizen-led community. The fact that "USonian
Journals 2000" was circulated widely as a "xeroxed and e-mailed pamphlet"
following the reelection of President George W. Bush in 2004 offers a direct
comment on the power of Rich's poetry to speak to people in times of political
uncertainty and to foster hope for liberatory politics (Werner, "Trying to Keep
Faith," 244).

Rich's next collection, *Telephone Ringing in the Labyrinth,* contains six
sections with poems written from 2004 to 2006, a time period that encompasses

an Iraqi-U.S. war, years of the Bush presidency, and Hurricane Katrina in New Orleans—all topics in the collection. The epigraphs to *Telephone Ringing in the Labyrinth* provide us with some insight into Rich's efforts to speak to readers. There she offers a quote from Alan Davies that he wrote in a review of Brenda Iijima's collection *Around Sea* in a poetry newsletter: *"Poetry isn't easy to come by. / You have to write it like you owe a debt to the world. / In that way poetry is how the world comes to be in you"* (TRL n.p.). This quote is followed by a line from Michael S. Harper from his book *Songlines in Michaeltree: New and Collected Poems: "Poetry is not self-expression, the I is a dramatic I"* (TRL n.p.). The page closes with a comment from Rich: *"To which I would add: and so, unless / otherwise indicated, is the You"* (TRL n.p.). Rich highlights her strategy for us here. The poems to be found in this *Telephone Ringing in the Labyrinth* are not just personal expressions or directed to an individual reader; rather the poems are purposefully created to raise larger issues, to draw out the world that is in each of us and around us.

This strategy clearly emerges in the poem "Calibrations," which opens with the image of a woman tuning her "guitar for Landstuhl / where she will sit on beds and sing / ballads from when Romany / roamed Spain" (TRL 17). Rich's notes to the collection tell us that Landstuhl is an American military hospital in Germany (TRL 105). This information changes the tenor of the poem, which heightens in the next lines:

> A prosthetic hand calibrates perfectly
> the stem of a glass
> or how to stroke a face
> is this how far we have come
> to make love easy (TRL 17)

The poem thrusts us into images not just of bodily loss but also of life and how life moves forward through technology. Despite the loss of limbs, there remains the desire for touch, for delicate sensations, which the prosthetics attempt to replicate. Yet the prosthetics cannot erase the loss of the limb; as the poem's speaker comments, "Ghost limbs go into spasm in the night / You come back from war with the body you have" (TRL 17). The line calls to mind December 2004, when U.S. Secretary of Defense Donald Rumsfeld, in response to a soldier's pleas for more armored vehicles, stated, "You go to war with the Army you have, not the Army you might want or wish to have at a later time" (Schmitt). In this way Rich situates the poem fully in the history of the Iraq war and calls readers' attention to the losses experienced by amputee veterans.

The poem continues onward, addressing the "you":

What you can't bear
carry endure lift
you'll have to drag

it'll come with you the ghostlimb

the shadow   blind
echo of your body spectre of your soul (TRL 17)

The poem asserts that the loss of the limb remains ever present haunting one's body. The poem's speaker shifts the tenor again, telling us, "Let's not talk yet of making love / nor of ingenious devices / replacing touch // And this is not theoretical: / A poem with calipers to hold a heart / so it will want to go on beating" (TRL 18). The poem refuses to allow us to focus in only on the loss of limbs or the rebuke to Rumsfeld for his callous response to soldiers asking for armor. Rather the poem deepens our understanding of the violence of war, while also giving hope for continuance. David Wojahn, in discussing the opening sequence poem in *An Atlas of the Difficult World,* notes that the power in Rich's poetry comes from the intimacy she develops between the written page and readers. He writes that "the intimacy of this transaction is seen by Rich as a fundamental source of poetry's transformative power. The poem does not so much develop this argument as it allows its force to deepen, thanks to the relentless particularity of its examples" (Wojahn 71). Readers experience such a deepening in "Calibrations" as they are taken from a seemingly innocent scene into a military hospital and into the minds of the amputees haunted by their "ghostlimbs." The poem then transitions into the ways in which people can carry on despite tremendous losses. The poem continues situated on "calipers," the metal supports to hold a leg, and keeps beating, thus suggesting the ability of the amputee to continue living.

   The challenge of *Telephone Ringing in the Labyrinth,* as with many of Rich's later poems, is the disjointed style the poems utilize. With fractured lines, allusions to current events and other writers, and fragmented images, these poems offer no answers or resolutions as could be found in her earlier work. As one reviewer comments, "If the collection does have a characteristic mode, it is that of montage—Rich creating a sense of expanded connectedness not by writing about connections, but by juxtaposing moments, glimpses, thought and feelings and leaving the reader to make the running" (Andrea). Increasingly, for readers to make sense of Rich's later work, the notes to each collection are an important tool to deciphering her poems, as we see with the poem "Letters Censored, Shredded, Returned to Sender or Judged Unfit to

Send," which is difficult to read without more contextual information. Rich's notes tell us that the italicized lines are from a book by Giuseppe Fiori on Antonio Gramsci, an Italian Marxist theoretician, as well as Gramsci's prison notebooks. Gramsci is recognized for his writings on cultural hegemony that examines how societies are governed by a ruling class that manipulates cultural values and beliefs to create an accepted way of viewing the world. This world-view then becomes the dominant worldview. Gramsci was imprisoned in 1926 by Mussolini's government for his political opposition and writings. He died in 1932 after six years of imprisonment that led to health issues.

The poem's epigraph quotes the prosecutor from Gramsci's sentencing: "*We must prevent this mind from functioning*" (TRL 65). The poem then inter-sperses quotes from Fiori and Gramsci, along with other fragments and images, in a disjointed pattern along with lines that include equations, such as "when consciousness + sensation feels like/ = suffering—" (TRL 66) and

$$—\text{History} = \text{bodies in time}—$$
or, in your language:
$$H = \underline{T}$$
$$B \text{ (TRL 68-9)}.$$

Rich's readers must piece together comments that vacillate between a fear of "this void, this vacuum" (TRL 67) and the need for language to push against cultural hegemony and to seek new ideas and ways of living, as seen in the poem's assertion, "The old structure does not contain and is unable / to satisfy the new needs" (TRL 69).

Rich picks up this theme again in "Rereading *The Dead Lecturer*," which references a collection of poems by the African American writer Amiri Baraka. The poem opens reaching back to the energies of past social movements: "An idea.   And we felt it. / A meaning.   And we caught it" (TRL 60). The poem reminisces about the power that came from such communal actions:

> Shed the dead hand,
> let sound be sense.   A world
> echoing everywhere, Fanon, Freire, thin pamphlets lining
> raincoat pockets, poetry on walls, damp purple mimeos cranking
> —the feeling of an idea.   An idea of feeling. (TRL 60)

Once again the reader needs historical context and must recognize the names Fanon and Freire, individuals known for their writings challenging dominant culture and ways of thinking. The poem recalls the energy that came from so-cial movements built on ideas and communal energy with a focus on the power of words. One can read the phrase "A world / echoing everywhere" as a word echoing where "sound be sense" and pamphlets and mimeos spread the "feeling of an idea" (TRL 60).

Other familiar Rich themes can be found in this collection. For example, in "Skeleton Key," Rich moves away from the personal, telling her readers, "this is how I came to be / protector of the private / and enemy of the personal" (TRL 19). The poem seeks to find a key, a "skeleton" key that can open any locked door to bring us back to "that city / talk starting up, deals and poetry // Tense with elation" (TRL 20). There, Rich seeks to recover connection and energy— the "revived boldness of cats / locked eyes of couples / music playing full blast again" (TRL 20). In "Hubble Photographs: After Sappho," readers encounter a depiction of love, "the person with whom you hope to live and die," juxtaposed with the vastness of the universe, the "body's cavity, violet green livid and venous / gorgeous" (TRL 50).

With "This Is Not the Room," Rich takes on the administration of America's forty-third president from 2001 to 2009, George W. Bush. The poem opens with an image of "polished tables lit with medalled / torsos bent toward microphones / where ears lean hands scribble / 'working the dark side'" (TRL 52). The phrase "working the dark side," as Rich's notes document, are from a comment made by the vice president of the United States at the time, Richard Cheney, on the television program *Meet the Press* on 16 September 2001, only five days after the bombings of the World Trade Center and the Pentagon and the downing of a plane over Pennsylvania. There, Cheney stated, "We also have to work, though, sort of the dark side, if you will. We've got to spend time in the shadows in the intelligence world. A lot of what needs to be done here will have to be done quietly, without any discussion, using sources and methods that are available to our intelligence agencies, if we're going to be successful. That's the world these folks operate in, and so it's going to be vital for us to use any means at our disposal, basically, to achieve our objective" (eMedia Millworks).

The poem, by referencing Vice President Cheney's statement, highlights American government practices in the days following the 9/11 terrorist attacks. The poem continues on to challenge these actions by calling into question the room the government works out of:

> This is not the room where tears down carven
> cheeks track rivulets in the scars
> left by the gouging tool
> where wood itself is weeping
>
> where the ancient painted eye speaks to the living eye
>
> This is the room

> where truth scrubs around the pedestal of the toilet
> flings her rag into the bucket
> straightens up   spits at the mirror (TRL 52)

Readers cannot miss Rich's disgust with shadowy government practices that use any means to an end. In *What Is Found There,* Rich comments on the shift in American foreign policy and the reaction to 9/11, a time when "private and public grief for civilian losses from many cultures and nations at the World Trade Center had to make way for the patriotic imperative to spend, consume, rescue the economy for profiteering and militarization, as fear was sowed broadside by our government as well as by lethal extremist acts" (WFT 261). In a 2003 essay, "Iraqi Poetry Today," Rich clearly states her position: "As an American poet, I see my country represented in Iraq by an inept and cruel military occupation, and by a government whose cultural insensibility, at home and abroad, is absolute" (*A Human Eye* 7). "This Is Not the Room" captures Rich's willingness to speak out against her government, to call into "sharper relief" a nation that had "been riven within and whirling in megalomaniac violence abroad and for a long time, fantasizing itself safe behind the electronic fences and stockpiled resources of a gated community" (WFT 261).

The collection concludes with the five-sequence title poem, "Telephone Ringing in the Labyrinth." Yet again readers are connected with a poem that asks more questions rather than providing answers. Is anyone picking up the telephone? Is poetry reaching anyone? What messages prevail and are heard? In the fifth poem of the sequence, Rich addresses not just her readers but also poetry itself, commenting that she

> Desired not
>
> you so much as your life,
> your prevailing   Not for me
> but for furtherance   how
>
> you would move
> on the horizon   You, the person, you
> the particle   fierce and furthering (TRL 103)

This is Rich in fine form, calling upon not just the power of poetry but also the actions of us, the readers, to prevail and further the world. In a review of *Telephone Ringing in the Labyrinth,* John Freeman comments that "in the 1980s and 1990s, [Rich] stretched her line to the breaking point, and turned outward, as Susan Sontag did in her essays, addressing the way the media and news push at the boundaries of the self, making us culpable—at least as Americans—for everything that happens from Beirut to Boston." Ultimately, *Telephone Ringing in the Labyrinth* exemplifies Rich's ongoing belief in language as the tool for making connections and for engaging the world. As she writes in "Wallpaper," "If the word gets out if the word / escapes if the word / flies as it dies / it has its way of coming back" (TRL 23).

Rich's final collection of poetry, *Tonight No Poetry Will Serve,* was published in 2011 and contains six sections. At the end of her lengthy career, Rich's final collection, like previous collections, returns to long-contemplated themes. The opening poem of the collection, "Waiting for Rain, for Music," draws in two quotes to set the tone. Rich's notes tell us that the first, "*Send my roots rain,*" is from the poet Gerard Manley Hopkins's work, while the second, "*A struggle at the roots of the mind,*" is from the writings of Raymond Williams, a cultural materialist (TNP 83). These lines call to mind Rich's persistent recognition of the need to keep interrogating the world and the struggle for poetry to be heard. In "You, Again," Rich explains that the "you" is "a personified city—New York as I knew and lived it in the sixties and seventies," and the poem "has to do with the recurrent longing for return and restoration" (Waldman). "Scenes of Negotiation," a longer prose poem that composes section 2, contemplates the individual and communal costs of oppression and the ongoing need for collective resistance.

"Tonight No Poetry Will Serve," the title poem of Rich's final poetry collection, frames the collection and speaks to Rich's ongoing concerns about the power of language to change the world. It is important to note that the collection's epigraph offers up varying definitions of the verb "to serve." According to Rich, the verb offers "an interesting range of meanings, from the idea of obedient servitude to the authoritative (from law, the military, a prison sentence), to the meeting of another's needs, to being of use" (Waldman). Each of these definitions places someone or something at the service of another. The poem begins with the image of someone barefoot gazing at the new moon and then "asleep but not oblivious / of the unslept unsleeping / elsewhere" (TNP 25). This image of someone sleeping yet connected to others through an awareness of another's suffering is juxtaposed with the second half of the poem where language itself comes under attack:

> verb pilots the plane
> adverb modifies action
>
> verb force-feeds noun
> submerges the subject

          noun is choking
          verb   disgraced   goes on doing (TNP 25)

In one sense, as Rich noted in an interview, the lines point to "an official grammar, parsing violent policies as you might diagram a sentence in a classroom" (Waldman). On another level the poem suggests Rich's larger concern with the ability of language to handle a world torn by war, terrorism, global power, violence. Language, here, is drowning and lacks meaning.

Rich recounts that the poem was impacted by "interviews I was hearing on Amy Goodman's program, *Democracy Now!*—about Guantánamo, waterboarding, official U.S. denials of torture, the 'renditioning' of presumed terrorists to countries where they would inevitably be tortured. The line 'Tonight I think no poetry will serve' suggests that no poetry can serve to mitigate such acts, they nullify language itself" (Waldman). In another interview Rich asked, "How can poetry, in its fullest sense, coexist with or even affect things like rendition and torture? Is it in service to them, how does it refuse service, how in fact resist?" (Richardson). In his review of the collection, Peter Erickson points out that the "angry command in the last line carries the sense of 'sentence' as inescapable judgment, conviction, and penalty," thus reinforcing Rich's interrogation of rendition and torture (106). The poem suggests that poetry might lack the power to impact war and torture, let alone exist in the face of such violence. Yet the poem's final line, "now diagram the sentence," suggests that we, the readers, may have an ability to break apart language to find what might serve us (TNP 25).

"Axel Avákar" makes up the fourth section of the collection and is composed of five poems. Rich explicated the poem in an interview, explaining that it depicts "two figures, once somehow intimately connected, now separated, one addressing the other, meeting silence or a recorded message. There are missed dialogues, lost opportunities, danger, the question of who can rescue whom. It's a densely layered scenario; I hope it resists reduction. I wanted a very visual, vocal sequence of places, emotions, situations" (Waldman). While Rich saw the much earlier poem "The Demon Lover" from the 1969 collection *Leaflets* as a predecessor to this poem, there are also clear linkings to "USonian Journals" from *Midnight Salvage,* in which similar misconnections and abnegation of responsibility exist. Further, the poem links back to Rich's ongoing concern with the shaping of self-identity in a world that often oppresses those efforts.

In "Poverties and Protest," a review of the collection, Christina Cook explains that in "Axel, in thunder," the third poem, the fictive Axel Avákar is isolated during a storm, a position not of his own choosing. In the face of the weather, he is "crawling exposed   not by choice," and Rich calls out to him,

"O my terrified   my obdurate / my wanderer   keep the trail" (TNP 45). Here, Cook notes that Axel "represents, among other things, the untold numbers of real men and women who are not at liberty to shape their own identity." This inability is highlighted by the sequence's fourth poem, "I was there, Axel," in which Rich pictures a woman who "walked on knives to gain a voice" as she "fished the lake of lost / messages" (TNP 46). The woman worked to haul in the messages, despite one arm being "tied behind her" (TNP 46). Rich then asserts,

> I was there Axel
> with her in that boat
>
> working alongside
>
> and my decision was
> to be in no other way
>
> a woman (TNP 46)

The poem forefronts an active claiming of identity, something Axel is unable to do. Further, "the speaker makes a strong claim of her own action and identity here, which the clipped lines and elliptical syntax promote: 'and my decision was' at first reads as if it refers to her decision of 'working alongside' the woman in the boat" (Cook).

Continuing on, the decision shifts to her assertion "to be in no other way / a woman." Grammatically and semantically, the "decision" refers to both what she is doing and who she is: a woman helping another woman to lift voices up out of the silence imposed upon them "from far below and long ago" (Cook). Familiar Rich themes arise here regarding the need for communal restoration of history, the "lost messages," as well as the need for bonds between women. At the same time, the poem is reminiscent of "Twenty-One Love Poems," which ends with Rich seeing herself as "more than stone: / a woman. I choose to walk here. And to draw this circle" (DCL 36), as well as the "Sources" sequence, in which she chooses her gender, her "powerful and womanly series of / choices," as her guide (YNL 27). Gender throughout Rich's career always played a central role.

The closing poem of the collection, "Powers of Recuperations," speaks to Rich's never-ending quest for social action, for collective resistance to violence, for communal responsibility, and for the imagining of new structures. Rich explicated the poem in an interview, something she did not often do throughout her career. There she explained, "that poem begins, 'A woman of the citizens' party,' and immediately a voice interrupts: 'What's that?' Implied is a forgotten history of radical citizenship, resistance, 'party' still existing but now banished, clandestine. Its former or future leaders are to be found living under bridges, communicating in codes, preparing another phase of history, a new learning. That woman might be a leader or a message-bearer, one of those who haven't given up, who move organically with what's required by new situations, seeming chaos" (Waldman).

In the poem the woman is "old, the incendiary / woman // endless beginner" (TNP 76). As the woman walks across a cityscape, she contemplates the resistance and oppression of the people: "those streets of minds / shuttered against shatter // articulate those walls / pronouncing rage and need" (TNP 78). In the poem's fourth section, the city's landscape of seven bridges is highlighted. Erickson reads these seven bridges as "an apparent reference to the problem of the seven bridges of Königsberg, which Leonhard Euler proved in 1736 could not be crossed in a single unrepeated circuit" (108). The poem suggests that the variation of routes is valuable, "for why would one want to be limited to one perfect route instead of the multiple possibilities" (Erickson 108).

The poem closes with an image that Rich explains is "from Dürer's famous engraving, *Melencolia I*. It shows a woman, powerful in face and body, introspective, seated among various instruments of science and artisanship. She seems to be imagining—we don't know what. *Melencolia I* refers to an old idea of the melancholy of the imaginative spirit—not sadness but a profound study of the world" (Waldman). The figure of the woman is a "massive figure on unrest's verge / pondering the unbuilt city // cheek on hand and glowing eyes and / skirted knees apart" (TNP 81). The woman sits on the edge of change, of imagining the new, with an energy represented by her glowing eyes and legs spread as if ready to move to action. Commenting on this closing image, Rich stated, "So walking through the desolation of a built city, the woman citizen encounters a figurative planner of the 'unbuilt place.' My hope is that these metaphorical creations don't stay metaphorical for too long" (Waldman). *Tonight No Poetry Will Serve* concludes by pushing readers forward to contemplate again what might be, what we might create in the future.

For Rich, creating a better future is ongoing work; more importantly, for Rich, poetry is the medium by which the work can take shape. As Rich continually reminds readers in *What Is Found There*, "Poetry is not a resting on the given, but a questing toward what might otherwise be" (234). Throughout her career Rich guided her readers to contemplate and create what "might otherwise be." This desire stemmed from her consistent belief that "poetic imagination or intuition is never merely unto itself, free-floating, or self-enclosed. It's radical, meaning root-tangled in the grit of human arrangements and relationships: *how we are with each other*" (*A Human Eye* 96). Rich's late work from 1999 tó 2011 urges readers to consider relationships, personal and public accountability, and how we can use language to connect. Further, while Rich recognized that "poetry is not a healing lotion, an emotional massage, a kind of linguistic aromatherapy. Neither is it a blueprint, nor an instruction manual, nor a billboard" (*Poetry and Commitment* 21), she also believed that "if there's a line to be drawn, it's not so much between secularism and belief as between those for whom language has metaphoric density and those for whom it is merely formulaic—to be used for repression, manipulation, empty certitudes to ensure obedience" (*Poetry and Commitment* 33).

Her later poems ask readers to hold on to the "metaphoric density" in language that poetry preserves, to remember that, as she wrote, "poetry has the capacity—in its own ways and by its own means—to remind us of something we are forbidden to see. A forgotten future: a still-uncreated site whose moral architecture is founded not on ownership and dispossession, the subjection of women, torture and bribes, outcast and tribe, but on the continuous redefining of freedom—that word now held under house arrest by the rhetoric of the 'free' market" (*Poetry and Commitment* 36). For Rich, poetry has always been the vehicle that can lead people to understand who they are and where they are located in history, particularly if the poem is written in a way that confronts readers, forcing them to question their surroundings. The poem that moves people, according to Rich, is a revolutionary poem. For Rich, a "revolutionary poem will not tell you who or when to kill, what or when to burn, or even how to theorize. It reminds you (for you have known, somehow, all along, maybe lost track) where and when and how you are living and might live—it is a wick of desire" (WFT 241).

Moreover, Rich explains that "truly revolutionary art is an alchemy through which waste, greed, brutality, frozen indifference, 'blind sorrow,' and anger are transmuted into some drenching recognition of the *What if?*—the possible. *What if—?*—the first revolutionary question, the question the dying forces don't know how to ask" (WFT 241). In a 1998 interview, Rich captured this sentiment, explaining that "poetry is liberative language, connecting the fragments within us, connecting us to others like and unlike ourselves, replenishing our desire. It's potentially catalytic speech because it's more than speech: it is associative, metaphoric, dialectical, visual, musical; in poetry words can say more than they mean and mean more than they say. In a time of frontal assaults both on language and on human solidarity, poetry can remind us of all we are in danger of losing—disturb us, embolden us out of resignation" (Prince).

In *Arts of the Possible,* Rich firmly asserts, "We're not simply trapped in the present. We are not caged within a narrowing corridor at 'the end of history.' Nor do any of us have to windsurf on the currents of a system that depends on the betrayal of so many others. We do have choices. We're living through a certain part of history that needs us to live it and make it and write it. We can make that history with many others, people we will never know. Or, we can live in default, under protest perhaps, but neutered in our senses and in our sympathies" (166–67). Rich throughout her career chose to make and write history. Along the way she challenged her readers to do the same. This is the power and legacy of Adrienne Rich.

BIBLIOGRAPHY

Works by Adrienne Rich

POETRY

A Change of World, with foreword by W. H. Auden. New Haven, Conn.: Yale University Press, 1951.

Poems. New York: Oxford University Poetry Society, 1952.

The Diamond Cutters and Other Poems. New York: Harper, 1955.

Snapshots of a Daughter-in-Law: Poems, 1954–1962. New York: Harper, 1963; revised edition, New York: W. W. Norton, 1967.

Necessities of Life. New York: W. W. Norton, 1966.

Selected Poems. London: Chatto & Windus, 1967.

Leaflets: Poems, 1965–1968. New York: W. W. Norton, 1969.

The Will to Change: Poems, 1968–1970. New York: W. W. Norton, 1971.

Diving into the Wreck, Poems 1971–72. New York: W. W. Norton, 1973.

Poems: Selected and New, 1950–1974. New York: W. W. Norton, 1974.

The Dream of a Common Language: Poems 1974–1977. New York: W. W. Norton, 1978; reissued, 1993.

A Wild Patience Has Taken Me This Far: Poems 1978–1981. New York: W. W. Norton, 1981; reissued, 1993.

Sources. Woodside, Calif.: Heyeck Press, 1983.

The Fact of a Doorframe: Poems Selected and New 1950–1984. New York: W. W. Norton, 1984.

Your Native Land, Your Life. New York: W. W. Norton, 1986.

Time's Power, Poems 1985–1988. New York: W. W. Norton, 1989.

An Atlas of the Difficult World: Poems 1988–1992. New York: W. W. Norton, 1991.

Collected Early Poems: 1950–1970. New York: W. W. Norton, 1993.

Dark Fields of the Republic: 1991–1995. New York: W. W. Norton, 1995.

Selected Poems, 1950–1995. Knockeven, Ireland: Salmon Publishers, 1996.

Midnight Salvage: Poems 1995–1998. New York: W. W. Norton, 1999.

Fox: Poems 1998–2000. New York: W. W. Norton, 2001.

The School among the Ruin: Poems 2000–2004. New York: W. W. Norton, 2004.

Telephone Ringing in the Labyrinth: Poems 2004–2006. New York: W. W. Norton, 2007.

Tonight No Poetry Will Serve: Poems 2007–2010. New York: W. W. Norton, 2011.

PROSE

Of Woman Born: Motherhood as Experience and Institution. New York: W. W. Norton, 1976; reissued with revised introduction, 1986.

Women and Honor: Some Notes on Lying (pamphlet). Pittsburgh: Motheroot Publishing/ Pittsburgh Women Writers, 1977.

On Lies, Secrets, and Silence: Selected Prose 1966–1978. New York: W. W. Norton, 1979.

Compulsory Heterosexuality and Lesbian Existence (pamphlet). Denver: Antelope Publications, 1980.

Blood, Bread, and Poetry: Selected Prose 1979–1985. New York: W. W. Norton, 1986.

What Is Found There: Notebooks on Poetry and Politics. 2nd edition. New York: W. W. Norton, 1999; reissued, 2003.

Arts of the Possible: Essays and Conversation. New York: W. W. Norton, 2001.

"Making the Connections." *The Nation.* 30 December 2002. Web. 12 May 2014.

Poetry and Commitment: An Essay. New York: W. W. Norton, 2007.

"Poetry and Experience: Statement at a Poetry Reading (1964)." In *Adrienne Rich's Poetry: Texts of the Poems, the Poet on Her Work; Reviews and Criticism*, ed. Barbara Charlesworth Gelpi and Albert Gelpi, 165. New York: W. W. Norton, 1975.

A Human Eye: Essays on Art in Society, 1997–2008. New York: W. W. Norton, 2009.

Secondary Sources

Andrea, Meredith. "Too Reflective, Too Fierce, Too Engaging." *Stride Magazine,* February 2008. Web. 4 November 2014.

Atwood, Margaret. "Review of *Diving into the Wreck.*" In *Adrienne Rich's Poetry: Texts of the Poems; the Poet on Her Work; Reviews and Criticism,* ed. Barbara Charlesworth Gelpi and Albert Gelpi, 277–79. New York: W. W. Norton, 1975.

Auden, W. H. "Foreword to *A Change of World.*" In *Adrienne Rich's Poetry: Texts of the Poems; the Poet on Her Work; Reviews and Criticism,* ed. Barbara Charlesworth Gelpi and Albert Gelpi, 125–26. New York: W. W. Norton, 1975.

Bell, Barbara Currier. "Cable of Blue Fire: Glimpsing a Group Identity for Humankind." *Studies in the Humanities* 15.2 (1988): 90–107.

Bennett, Paula. *My Life, a Loaded Gun: Female Creativity and Feminist Poetics.* Boston: Beacon Press, 1986.

Benson, Heidi. "In a World of Violence, Inequality and Moral Chaos, Adrienne Rich's Voice Will Be Neither Silent nor Content." *San Francisco Chronicle,* 29 March 2005. Web, 14 October 2014.

Boland, Eavan. "When a Couplet Caught Fire—The Poetry of Adrienne Rich." *New Republic,* 9 November 2012. Web, 27 July 2014.

Bundtzen, Lynda K. "Adrienne Rich's Identity Poetics: A Partly Common Language." *Women's Studies* 27.4 (1998): 331–45.

Campo, Rafael. "Exemplary Poet." *The Progressive* 63.7 (1999): 43–44.

———. "A Gift of Love and Light." *Nation* 263.6 (1996): 25–26.

Cook, Christina. "Poverties and Protest: *Tonight No Poetry Will Serve: Poems 2007–2010.*" *Cerise Press: A Journal of Literature, Arts, and Culture* 3.7 (2011): n.p. Web, 8 November 2014.

Des Pres, Terrence. *Praises and Dispraises: Poetry and Politics in the Twentieth Century.* New York: Viking, 1988.

DeShazer, Mary K. "'The End of a Century': Feminist Millennial Vision in Adrienne Rich's *Dark Fields of the Republic.*" *NWSA Journal* 8.3 (1996): 37–62.

Diehl, Joanne Feit. "'Cartographies of Silence': Rich's Common Language and the Woman Poet." In *Reading Adrienne Rich: Reviews and Revisions, 1951–1981,* ed. Roberta Cooper, 91–110. Ann Arbor: University of Michigan Press, 1984.

————. *Women Poets and the American Sublime.* Bloomington: Indiana University Press, 1990.

Doty, Mark. Afterword. In Adrienne Rich, *Poetry and Commitment.* New York: W. W. Norton, 2007.

Eagleton, Mary. "Adrienne Rich, Location and the Body." *Journal of Gender Studies* 9.3 (2000): 299–312.

Eliot, T. S. *Selected Prose of T. S. Eliot.* Ed. Frank Kermode. New York: Harcourt Brace Jovanovich, 1975.

eMedia Millworks. "Text: Vice President Cheney on NBC's Meet the Press." *Washington Post,* 16 September 2001. Web, 14 November 2014.

Erickson, Peter. "Tonight No Poetry Will Serve: Poems, 2007–2010." *Women's Studies* 41.1 (2012): 105–8.

Erkkila, Betsy. *The Wicked Sisters: Women Poets, Literary History, and Discord.* New York: Oxford University Press, 1992.

Flood, Allison. "Adrienne Rich, Award Winning Poet and Essayist, Dies Aged 82." *Guardian,* 29 March 2012. Web, 30 November 2012.

Fox, Margalit. "A Poet of Unswerving Vision at the Forefront of Feminism." *New York Times,* 28 March 2012. Web, 30 November 2012.

Freeman, John. "In 'Telephone Ringing,' Adrienne Rich Makes Music of Words." *SF-Gate.* 30 December 2007. Web. 10 August 2014.

Friedan, Betty. *The Feminine Mystique.* New York: W. W. Norton, 1963.

Gelpi, Albert. "Adrienne Rich: The Poetics of Change." In *Adrienne Rich's Poetry: Texts of the Poems; the Poet on Her Work; Reviews and Criticism,* ed. Barbara Charlesworth Gelpi and Albert Gelpi, 130–47. New York: W. W. Norton, 1975.

————. "Poetics of Recovery: A Reading of Adrienne Rich's *Sources.*" In *Adrienne Rich's Poetry: Texts of the Poems; the Poet on Her Work; Reviews and Criticism,* ed. Barbara Charlesworth Gelpi and Albert Gelpi, 397–401. New York: W. W. Norton, 1975.

Gelpi, Barbara Charlesworth, and Albert Gelpi. *Adrienne Rich's Poetry: Texts of the Poems; the Poet on Her Work; Reviews and Criticism.* New York: W. W. Norton, 1975.

Gilbert, Sandra, and Susan Gubar. *The Madwoman in the Attic: The Woman Writer and the Nineteenth Century.* New Haven, Conn.: Yale University Press, 1979.

Greenwald, Elissa. "The Dream of a Common Language: Vietnam Poetry as Reformation of Language and Feeling in the Poems of Adrienne Rich." *Journal of American Culture* 16.3 (1993): 97–102.

Grimstad, Kristen, and Susan Rennie, eds. *The New Woman's Survival Sourcebook.* New York: Knopf, 1975.

Grosz, Elizabeth. *Volatile Bodies.* Bloomington: Indiana University Press, 1994.

Gwiazda, Piotr. "'Nothing Else Left to Read': Poetry and Audience in Adrienne Rich's *An Atlas of the Difficult World.*" *Journal of Modern Literature* 28.2 (2005): 165–88.

Hall, Donald. "A Diet of Dissatisfaction." In *Reading Adrienne Rich: Reviews and Revisions, 1951–1981,* ed. Roberta Cooper, 212–14. Ann Arbor: University of Michigan Press, 1984.

Harris, Virginia Frankel. "Imagine That—Reform(ulat)ing a World of Pain." In *Reconstructing Pain & Joy: Linguistic, Literary, & Cultural Perspectives,* ed. Chryssoula Lascaratou, Ann Despotopoulou, and Elly Ifantidou, 135–56. Newcastle: Cambridge Scholars Publishing, 2008.

Hart, George. "The Long Line in Rich's Recent Poetry." *Women's Studies* 27.1 (1998): 397–411.

Henneberg, Sylvia. *The Creative Crone: Aging and the Poetry of May Sarton and Adrienne Rich.* Columbia: University of Missouri Press, 2010.

Hussmann, Mary. "On Adrienne Rich." *Iowa Review* 22.1 (1992): 221–25.

Jarrell, Randall. "Review of *The Diamond Cutters and Other Poems.*" In *Adrienne Rich's Poetry: Texts of the Poems; the Poet on Her Work; Reviews and Criticism,* ed. Barbara Charlesworth Gelpi and Albert Gelpi, 127–29. New York: W. W. Norton, 1975.

Juhasz, Suzanne. *Naked and Fiery Forms: Modern American Poetry by Women, a New Tradition.* New York: Harper & Row, 1976.

Keyes, Claire. *The Aesthetic of Power: The Poetry of Adrienne Rich.* Athens: University of Georgia Press, 1986.

Klein, Michael. "A Rich Life: Adrienne Rich on Poetry, Politics, and Personal Revelation." *Boston Phoenix,* June 1999. Web, 25 August 2014.

Langdell, Cheryl Colby. *Adrienne Rich: The Moment of Change.* Westport, Conn.: Praeger, 2004.

Martin, Wendy. *An American Triptych: Anne Bradstreet, Emily Dickinson, Adrienne Rich.* Chapel Hill: University of North Carolina Press, 1984.

McDaniel, Judith. "'Reconstituting the World': The Poetry and Vision of Adrienne Rich." In *Adrienne Rich's Poetry and Prose,* ed. Barbara Charlesworth Gelpi and Albert Gelpi, 310–21. New York: W. W. Norton, 1993.

Meese, Elizabeth. "Adrienne Rich." In *Modern American Critics since 1955,* ed. Gregory S. Jay, 232–40. *Dictionary of Literary Biography,* vol. 67. Detroit: Gale Research, 1988. Web, 25 March 2012.

———. *(Ex)Tensions: Re-Figuring Feminist Criticism.* Urbana: University of Illinois Press, 1990.

Montenegro, David. *Points of Departure: International Writers on Writing and Politics.* Ann Arbor: University of Michigan Press, 1991.

Morris, Adalaide. "Imitations and Identities: Adrienne Rich's *A Change of World.*" *Modern Poetry Studies* 10.2,3 (1981): 136–59.

Moyers, Bill. *The Language of Life: A Festival of Poets.* New York: Anchor, 1996.

Oktenberg, Adrian. "Disloyal to Civilization: The *Twenty-One Love Poems* of Adrienne Rich." In *Reading Adrienne Rich: Reviews and Re-Visions, 1951–81,* ed. Jane Roberta Cooper, 72–90. Ann Arbor: University of Michigan Press, 1984.

Orr, David. "Adrienne Rich, beyond the Anger." *New York Times,* 30 March 2012. Web, 1 April 2012.

Plumly, Stanley. "Talking with Adrienne Rich." *Ohio Review* 13.1 (1971): 29–46.

Poetry Foundation. "Adrienne Rich." 28 March 2012. Web, 1 April 2012.

Pollit, Katha. "Adrienne Rich's News in Verse." *New Yorker,* 30 March 2012. Web, 1 April 2012.

Pope, Deborah. *A Separate Vision: Isolation in Contemporary Women's Poetry.* Baton Rouge: Louisiana State University Press, 1984.

Prince, Ruth E. C. "The Possibilities of an Engaged Art: An Interview with Adrienne Rich." *Radcliffe Quarterly* (Fall 1998): n.p. Web, 30 September 2006.

Richardson, Cat. Interview with Adrienne Rich. *National Book Foundation.* n.d. Web, 2 December 2014.

Rothschild, Matthew. "Adrienne Rich: 'I happen to think poetry makes a huge difference.'" *The Progressive* 58.1 (1994): 31. *Expanded Academic ASAP.* Web, 9 October 2006.

St. John, David. "Brightening the Landscape." *Los Angeles Times,* 25 February 1996. Web, 1 April 2012.

Schmitt, Eric. "Iraq-Bound Troops Confront Rumsfeld over Lack of Armor." *New York Times,* 8 December 2004. Web, 14 November 2014.

Scully, James. *Line Break: Poetry as Social Practice.* Willimantic, Conn.: Curbstone Press, 2005.

Slowik, Mary. "The Friction of the Mind: The Early Poetry of Adrienne Rich." *Massachusetts Review: A Quarterly of Literature* 25.1 (1984): 142–60.

Stimpson, Catherine. "Adrienne Rich and Lesbian/Feminist Poetry." *Parnassus* 12.2–13.1 (1985): 249–68.

Templeton, Alice. "Contradictions: Tracking Adrienne Rich's Poetry." *Tulsa Studies in Women's Literature* 12.2 (1993): 333–40.

———. *The Dream and the Dialogue: Adrienne Rich's Feminist Poetics.* Knoxville: University of Tennessee Press, 1994.

Vendler, Helen. *Soul Says: On Recent Poetry.* Cambridge: Belknap Press of Harvard University Press, 1995.

Waddell, William. "Where We See It From: Adrienne Rich and a Reconstruction of American Space." In *'Catch if You Can Your Country's Moment': Recovery and Regeneration in the Poetry of Adrienne Rich,* ed. William Waddell, 81–100. Cambridge: Cambridge Scholars Press, 2007.

Waldman, Kate. "Adrienne Rich on *Tonight No Poetry Will Serve.*" *Paris Review,* 2 March 2011. Web, 15 October 2014.

Werner, Craig. *Adrienne Rich: The Poet and Her Critics.* Chicago: American Library Association, 1988.

———. "Trying to Keep Faith: Adrienne Rich's 'USonian Journals 2000.'" *Virginia Quarterly Review* 82.2 (2006): 241–46.

Whelchel, Marianne. "Mining the 'Earth-Deposits': Women's History in Adrienne Rich's Poetry." In *Reading Adrienne Rich: Reviews and Revisions, 1951–1981,* ed. Roberta Cooper, 51–71. Ann Arbor: University of Michigan Press, 1984.

Wojahn, David. "*An Atlas of the Difficult World:* 'Where Are We Moored? What Are the Bindings? What Behooves Us?'" *Field: Contemporary Poetry and Poetics* 77 (Fall 2007): 67–71.

Yorke, Liz. *Adrienne Rich: Passion, Politics, and the Body.* London: Sage, 1991.

INDEX

ABOUT THE AUTHOR

JEANNETTE E. RILEY is a professor of English, gender and women's studies at the University of Rhode Island. Riley's research focuses on women's literature, with an emphasis on contemporary women writers and feminist theory. Her writings on Adrienne Rich have appeared in *"Catch if you can your country's moment": Recovery and Regeneration in the Poetry of Adrienne Rich*, *From Motherhood to Mothering: The Legacy of Adrienne Rich's Of Woman Born*, and *Soundings: An Interdisciplinary Journal*.

"An important contribution to understanding and appreciating one of our truly great voices."

—MARGARET RANDALL,
author of *She Becomes Time* and
*Haydée Santamaría, Cuban Revolutionary:
She Led by Transgression*

"An ideal introduction for general readers and a solid foundation for future critical conversations."

—CRAIG WERNER,
author of *Adrienne Rich: The Poet
and Her Critics*

THE JOURNEY OF AN IMPORTANT FEMINIST WRITER THROUGH POETRY, PROSE, AND POLITICS

Among the most celebrated American poets of the past half century, Adrienne Rich was the recipient of numerous awards, including the Bollingen Prize, the National Book Award, and the Lannan Lifetime Achievement Award. In *Understanding Adrienne Rich*, Jeannette E. Riley assesses the full scope of Rich's career from 1957 to her death in 2012 through a chronological exploration of her poetry and prose.

Riley details the evolution of Rich's feminist poetics as she investigated issues of identity, sexuality, gender, the desire to reclaim women's history, and what she terms "the dream of a common language." Throughout the book she documents Rich's gradually developing assertion that poetry can create social change and engage people in the democratic process. Interweaving explications of Rich's poetry with analysis of her prose, Riley offers a close look at the development of the author's voice from formalist poet to feminist visionary to citizen poet.

JEANNETTE E. RILEY is professor of English and gender and women's studies at the University of Rhode Island. Her writings on Adrienne Rich have appeared in edited collections dedicated to Rich's work and in *Soundings: An Interdisciplinary Journal*.

Understanding Contemporary American Literature
Linda Wagner-Martin, series editor

Cover photograph: *Adrienne Rich, Santa Cruz, Ca.*, by Robert Giard, Photography Collection, Miriam and Ira D. Wallach Division of Art, Prints, and Photographs, The New York Public Library, Astor, Lenox, and Tilden Foundations. © Estate of Robert Giard.

Discover more books of interest at uscpress.com

LITERARY STUDIES

ISBN 978-1-64336-526-8